THE BUDDHA WALKS INTO A BAR

# THE BUDDHA WALKS INTO A BAR . . .

## A GUIDE TO LIFE FOR A NEW GENERATION

Lodro Rinzler

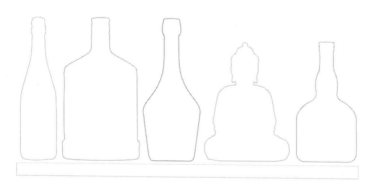

Shambhala / Boston & London / 2012

Shambhala Publications, Inc.
Horticultural Hall
300 Massachusetts Avenue
Boston, Massachusetts 02115
www.shambhala.com

9 8 7 6 5 4 3 2 1

First Edition
Printed in the United States of America

⊗This edition is printed on acid-free paper that meets the American
National Standards Institute Z39.48 Standard.
♲This book is printed on 30% postconsumer recycled paper. For
more information please visit www.shambhala.com.

Distributed in the United States by Random House, Inc.,
and in Canada by Random House of Canada Ltd

Library of Congress Cataloging-in-Publication Data
Rinzler, Lodro.
The Buddha walks into a bar: a guide to life for a new generation /
Lodro Rinzler.
p.   cm.
ISBN 978-1-59030-937-7 (pbk.: alk. paper)
1. Spiritual life—Buddhism. I. Title.
BQ5660.R56 2012
294.3′444—dc22
2011014498

For my Sakyong

# CONTENTS

## PART FOUR: RELAXING INTO MAGIC

# ACKNOWLEDGMENTS

Thank you. I mean that: your reading this book is a pretty big deal to me. My parents, Beth and Carl Rinzler, are wonderful and I owe them more than I could describe, and definitely more than I can describe in an acknowledgment page of a book. Victoria Gerstman, my lady, has been so supportive during this whole process and believed in me when I was sure this thing would never happen. She is really, really awesome. I love her and am so glad she has agreed to be my wife. I also want to thank my sister, Jane Buckingham, and my brother, Michael Rinzler, both of whom have always offered me nothing but encouragement and love.

I am blessed with many friends who have provided inspiration and support for this book (or, at the very least, bought me a beer and chewed my ear off about it): David Delcourt, Brett Eggleston, Oliver Tassinari, Ethan Nichtern, Will Conkling, Josh Silberstein, Laura Sinkman, Maron Greenleaf, Alex Okrent, David Perrin, Jeff Grow, Ericka Phillips, Marina Klimasiewfski, and the UsGuys. There are many other friends I should name and if you wonder why you're not on this list please know I hold you in my heart and thank you.

I have had two companions who were constantly looking over my shoulder, literally, while I wrote this book on my couch in Brooklyn. They are Tillie and Justin Bieber and they are very cute animals. As such they cannot read but I want to thank them for their warmth anyway.

Mentors are important and I have had the very best in Richard Reoch, Connie Brock, and Mitchell Levy. Thank you for your unwavering attention to detail and great care. Along the same lines, I want to thank Stan Lee for providing me with excellent role models growing up: the X-Men and Spider-Man.

I owe an incredible debt of gratitude to everyone at Shambhala Publications. I want to offer a thank-you to Sara Bercholz, for believing in this project and understanding it, sometimes better than I did. My gratitude goes out to Emily Bower, for nudging this in the right direction, and to Katie Keach and Ben Gleason, who both have a way of taking my words and transforming them into something eloquent. And of course, a big thank-you to Dave O'Neal for carefully editing this book and adding layers upon layers of clarity to it. It has been a joy to work with you all.

Acharya Adam Lobel has written extensively on the four dignities in manuals describing the *Way of Shambhala* curriculum. Alongside traditional source material, the images and language he used stuck with me and inspired me deeply. Last but certainly not least, none of the work in these pages would be here if I wasn't continuously inspired by the example of Sakyong Mipham Rinpoche, who I find to be the most genuine human being on the planet. Thank you all for making this possible.

# INTRODUCTION

This isn't your grandmother's book on meditation. It's for you. That is, assuming you like to have a beer once in a while, enjoy sex, have figured out that your parents are crazy, or get frustrated at work. It's a book that doesn't put Buddhism on some pedestal so that you have to look up to it. It's about looking at all the nooks and crannies of your life and applying Buddhist teachings to them, no matter how messy that may be.

Do you have to become Buddhist to like this book? Hell, no. Whatever wisdom lies within these pages is a result of excellent instruction on the part of my teachers and my own process of trial and error. The Buddhist dharma, or teaching, is not meant to be looked at as some obscure tome that needs to be dissected and analyzed. It is meant to be lived. So don't feel like you have to be Buddhist to get into this thing, you just have to have lived a little and be willing to look at your life from a new point of view.

Next question: Do you have to change your life to live the truths of this book? Hell, no, again. This book is for anyone who has ever said, "I'm spiritual," or "If I'm anything, I'm Buddhist." It's about taking these traditional teachings that have been tried and tested over thousands of years and saying, "I am going to try to live my day with a bit more compassion," or, "I'm going to slow down a bit and enjoy my life." You don't have to change *you*. You are great. This book is just about how to live your life to the fullest.

In it we explore the four dignities of Shambhala and the three *yanas*, or vehicles, of traditional Tibetan Buddhism. I'll offer what I know, but the rest is up to you. It is you who has to go out and live your life with mindfulness and compassion. You already know this. After all, true wisdom comes from within you. What this book provides is a series of tools to access that wisdom. We'll get into simple practices, advice, and teachings that can help you align yourself with your personal moral compass, the dignity of your own heart.

So if you want to be more in the "now," read this book. If you want to change the world, read this book. If you want to be a meditator and still enjoy a good drink, read this book. I wrote it for you. When you're done, drop me a line. I truly want to hear what you think.

*Lodro Rinzler*
*June 2, 2011*

## Part One

# FIRST, GET YOUR ACT TOGETHER

# 1 / YOUR LIFE IS A PLAYGROUND

⟶ warrior

If you have not tamed the enemy of your own anger
Combating outer opponents will only make them multiply.
Therefore, with an army of loving-kindness and compassion,
To tame your own mind is the practice of a Bodhisattva.

—*Ngulchu Thogme*

When I was young I had an alarm clock shaped like a Japanese samurai, with a sword in his hand and a clock in his belly. For the ten years it worked, I would wake up every morning with the sound of a warrior yelling in Japanese, "Wake up! Wake up! It is time for the battle!"

For many of us, life does feel like a battle. Our first instinct in the morning is one of self-protection, wanting to burrow back under the covers instead of facing the day. This is because we often view our daily routine as just a way to get by in life—pay the bills, find a romantic relationship, maintain our friendships, nurture our family life—and at the end of the day we are exhausted by our struggle to keep it all together.

We spend so much energy constantly trying to keep up with voice mail, e-mail, junk mail, bill mail, females, or males. Instead of engaging these various aspects of our life with an open mind, we schlep our way through them and cling to our escapes: we chew our nails, drink beer, have sex, shop online, or go to the gym. Some of us might even be able to multitask and do all of the above at once. Although we try our hardest, we know that at the end of the day there is always another thing we should do, and yet we have taken so little time to take care of ourselves.

This is when meditation is especially useful. Meditation practice is first and foremost about learning to be present and appreciate the world around us. It helps us view the world not as a battlefield, but as fertile ground to practice being openhearted and awake. Buddhist teachings show us that the only thing keeping us from being truly present with our world is a strong hang-up on our habitual way of looking at things.

Most of us have a set routine that gets us through our day. Somewhere along the line, we solidified that routine into a way of life. The question then becomes, "Is it working?" Day by day, we may find ourselves getting restless with the same classes or job, the same relationship, the same hangouts or hang-ups, and we long for some radical change.

However, it is not our world that is necessarily problematic; it's our point of view. It has been said that enlightenment is merely things as they are before we color them with our hopes and fears. If we could relax our idea of the way things should be and appreciate them as they are, then the world would be magically transformed into a rich ground of possibilities.

In the years I have been teaching Buddhism, I have often been struck by the incredible diversity in the sort of people who show up on the doorstep of meditation centers. Despite race, age, or economic class, the one unifying factor seems to be that none of them are entirely satisfied with their life as it currently stands. More often than not, they have tried everything else to make life more fulfilling—the new drug, the new job, the new car, the new romance—and yet none of it has brought a happily-ever-after scenario.

The Buddhist word for the cycle of suffering we find ourselves in is *samsara.* Samsara is everything from being uncomfortable because you have a hangnail, all the way to losing a beloved friend or family member. It is the fact that we long for what we don't have, and that makes us unhappy. It is the fact that when we get what we longed for, we're already thinking about something new that could entertain us.

Samsara is fueled by hope and fear. We hope we will do well at work, but fear we'll upset our boss. We hope to go to the beach, but fear rain. Extreme hope and fear can sometimes ruin an experience because we have spent so much time in our head agonizing over what could possibly happen. Having acknowledged that external factors may not bring lasting happiness, most people are inspired to look within for change, but most of us have no idea how to begin.

This general dissatisfaction is what the Buddha taught about when he opened his mouth for his first sermon ever. He didn't say, "Here's the plan, guys. Do X, Y, and Z, and you too will glow just like me." Instead he said, "Listen. You guys are unhappy, right? Let's analyze that." He then went on to point out that we suffer because we don't know much about who we are. The good news is that he said there can be a cessation to this whole restless-life syndrome and he laid out a path for us to explore ourselves and find our own way to awakening the heart and mind. That path is one of meditation and good conduct.

Meditation is a simple tool for self-reflection, yet it has tremendous power. While it does not offer you the cure-all to transform your life, meditation definitely has the power to transform your mind and heart, making them more expansive and more able to accommodate the obstacles you face on a daily basis. The more expansive your mind and heart, the more you are able to engage your world without life feeling like a battle.

There are three stages people go through as they enter into meditation practice. The first one could be described as the "Where did all these thoughts come from?" phase. We are so used to our hectic way of life that the simple act of

wisdom/compassion

sitting down to meditate and being present with our breath shows us that a waterfall of thoughts is pouring through us at light speed. We have never taken the time before to look inward, and it is shocking to find the quickly shifting tones of passion, anger, confusion, loneliness, and multiple variations thereof going through our head.

The basic technique of meditation is to take an upright posture, connect with our body, and focus our mind on the breath. The breath serves as an anchor, lodging us in this very moment, the present experience. That sounds simple enough, but after a few moments we begin to notice our mind drifting off to a conversation we had earlier that day, or forming a checklist of things we need to do the moment we are done meditating. When these thoughts come up, we are instructed to acknowledge them, not as good or bad, but just as thoughts, and bring our attention back to the physical sensation of the breath. If it is helpful, we can even mentally say "thinking" to ourselves in order to acknowledge that we are not doing anything horrible, and that we have the ability to return to the breath.

In one half-hour meditation session, we could have a wide variety of thoughts. Often in the "Where did all these thoughts come from?" phase, people get frustrated because they feel like they are not getting anywhere or that meditation does not work for them. Meditation has worked for numerous average-Joes-turned-meditation-masters over thousands of years, but you, you're most likely hopeless, right?

One of the beautiful things about Buddhism is that it does not worship Buddha as a god or deity, but instead celebrates the Buddha as an example of a normal person like you and me who applied a good deal of discipline and gentleness to his meditation practice, and ended up opening his mind and heart in a very big way.

When the Buddha was in his twenties, he wasn't some great enlightened master. His name was Siddhartha Gautama, and he lived at home with his father. He had a wife that he married at an early age, and before he knew it they had a son. He was also just discovering how sheltered he had been growing up, because it was only in his twenties that he first encountered suffering in the form of sickness, old age, and death. Not unlike most of us in our twenties, he didn't like what he saw in the world, and endeavored to find a way to change it.

Siddhartha Gautama, who I imagine was known as "Sid" by close friends and family, was inspired to pursue a spiritual life away from home. He went to great extremes to starve himself and live in harsh conditions in the name of holiness, as if he wanted a radical change from his cushy upbringing. Ultimately he discovered that by not being too indulgent or too hard on himself, he could tread a middle way where he could be kind to himself, practice meditation diligently, and live a noble life. Only then was he able to attain enlightenment.

Whenever people in the "Where did all these thoughts come from?" phase ask me what to do about their meditation practice, I recall what my teachers have told me: "Keep sitting." This is not some trip about having faith because a guy named Sid did it twenty-six hundred years ago, or because we can turn to people within meditation communities and see that others have benefited greatly from this practice. It is because we can see the effects of meditation ourselves.

When the Buddha attained enlightenment, he sought out close friends who had meditated with him in the past. Instead of approaching them with the mentality of "I've figured it out, now come study with me," he simply said, "Come and see for yourself."

Meditation is a path of self-discovery. If we take the advice of the Buddha and other great teachers from the past and continue to practice meditation, we too begin to move away from feeling like we are being bombarded by a waterfall of thoughts. Instead, it may feel more like we are in the midst of a very powerful thought river. This is not a bad start. Over time and with practice, it feels like the thoughts

*mediocre*

bombarding us are more at the pace of a babbling brook or gentle stream, which ultimately leads to the mind of wakefulness—a large spacious pond without a ripple on it.

The gradual process of getting accustomed to returning to our breath during meditation practice begins to develop some mental space, which over time, without us having to "do" anything at all, naturally begins to manifest in our daily life. In our meditation practice, we learn to acknowledge our thoughts without acting on them. This is an incredibly helpful tool when we live in a world where one angry e-mail or one delete button on a cell phone can end a relationship.

Perhaps during a meditation session we find ourselves angry with a coworker or classmate. We run through a number of pretend conversations with this person and tell them off in a different way each time. We analyze exactly how they wronged us in the past, and think of how we could get even. Each time we catch ourselves doing this during our meditation practice, we acknowledge it, label it "thinking," and return to the breath. It may run something like this:

"Brett is a real asshole."
"Thinking."
Back to the breath.
"Brett really went out of his way to ruin my morning didn't he? I bet he planned to—"
"Thinking."
Back to the breath.

By repeating this simple practice of allowing space on the meditation cushion, we are preparing to relate to this emotion and this person in our daily life. It is called "meditation practice" because we are practicing being present with our experience during meditation, and this practice spills over into the twenty-three-and-a-half hours we are not formally meditating. Hopefully the next time we see Brett, instead of buying into our habitual response of lashing out at him, we will encounter a small gap of spaciousness, a chance to not react as we always have in the past, and we will be able to just be present with whatever situation arises.

When we have such an experience, we may have graduated to the second phase, the "This thing actually helps me a little" phase. We are slightly tickled that meditation is starting to allow us to access more expansiveness in our mind and daily life. This is because meditation practice is not about trying to live up to some ideal version of who we are, but instead is about just being with ourselves and our experience, whatever it may be.

The third phase can be referred to as the "Meditation is like crack" phase. We have seen that by creating a more spacious situation around the thoughts and strong emotions affecting us in our meditation practice, we are more available to relate to them fully in our daily life. That feels good. So good that we want to continue to explore this path in the hope that we can bring some sense of sanity to ourselves, our daily life, and the world around us.

However, just like it took our prime example the Buddha many years to find a technique that worked for him, we cannot expect meditation to change our life overnight. If you want to get your body in shape, you don't expect a radical difference after a few days of running or a long weekend at the gym. Instead you start off slowly by getting accustomed to the weights and machines, building your strength session by session over a good deal of time. You feel inspired each time you are able to push yourself just a little more.

The same rule applies to our mind in meditation. We cannot expect to sit down for five hours and get enlightened. Nor should we sit fifteen minutes a day for a week, and when we feel that we are no more sane or openhearted than before, give up. Session by session, we begin to build up the mental flexibility and openness that make our mind hearty and strong. We need to start by training our mind regularly in short sessions, in order to build up the stability that eventually spills over into the rest of our lives.

Ultimately I believe that anyone attracted to a spiritual life wants to be of benefit to the world. No one picked up this book because they want a better car or better-looking partner. We want to learn how to be sane, how to be more openhearted in our daily lives, and how to spread sanity and compassion in an increasingly chaotic world. The first step is encountering our mental demons through getting to know ourselves in meditation. We need to befriend ourselves, and as cliché as it sounds, love ourselves, so that we can be available to love the world.

The samurai alarm clock points to one way we can approach our day. Every morning we can wake up and think, "It's time for the battle. Me versus the world." In order to win, we can be ruthless at work and get raises and promotions, buy the hottest new gadgets, and have a super-model spouse. That point of view gets old and exhausting, because we are constantly struggling to reach that new rung on the ladder of our career, our gadgets are outdated in months, and our partner's looks ultimately fade. Viewing our day as a battle separates us from the world around us, and makes it appear that our daily lives are something that we need to conquer, subjugate, or just survive.

Instead you can view your life as a rich opportunity. When the alarm clock goes off, you can take a minute to reflect on everything you have in your life—your friends, family, whatever you care about—and appreciate it. As you enter your day, you could take some time to meditate, and watch how taking that little bit of time for you makes you feel more spacious and your mind more expansive.

If you do this, you may find that the world that previously seemed so intimidating, so worth fighting against, is not as difficult when you don't bring your fixed passion, aggression, and confusion to each scenario, and instead infuse each new situation with spaciousness. The less we buy into our set version of how things should be, the more we can be available to things as they are. When we are able to do this, our lives are not a battle, but a playground for us to enjoy.

# 2 / LAUGH AT THE DISPLAY OF YOUR MIND

Before embarking on a path of developing our wisdom and compassion, we need to learn the basics. We need to learn how to work with our own mind. The meditation technique introduced in this chapter is commonly referred to as *shamatha*. *Shamatha* is a Sanskrit word that can be translated as "calm-abiding." That sounds pretty appealing, no? Just the process of taking time away from your speedy daily routine might induce this calming effect.

I should offer full disclosure, though: meditation does not always feel calm. When you begin to meditate, you will notice that shamatha has a shocking side effect, where you begin to see all the various aspects of your mind played out as if on a movie screen. You see your hopes, fears, and wildest sexual fantasies on a constant loop in your mind. After sitting with that loop for a while, you may discover that it's actually quite boring and repetitive. The thing is, it's always been there. You've just never looked directly at it.

## TRAINING THE MIND WITH SHAMATHA

Shamatha trains the mind in coming back to whatever is going on right now. When you are watching the display of your mind, and it cuts to a scene of how you could be in the Caribbean sipping a drink on a tropical beach and dipping your toes in the sand, you may realize, "Hey! That's not my reality. My reality is this too-cramped apartment, a bit of pain in my back, and a wandering mind." Believe it or not, this is a good thing. Noticing that you are lost in thought is the first step in coming back to the present on a regular basis.

It's a bit like the first step of Alcoholics Anonymous, where you admit that you are powerless over alcohol. Here you are saying, "I am powerless over this weird display of thoughts and emotions playing out in front of me." Just like in AA, though, there is a path to gain power, and this is through gently coming back to something other than your force of habit.

Learning shamatha meditation is like wielding a sword: you are able to cut through these discursive loops playing out in your mind as if you were cutting paper. Through continuously coming back to your breath, you learn that you don't have to get hooked by the fresh drama of the day. Instead you can touch in with the peaceful element behind all the madness: your own innate wisdom.

Meditation is practiced by traditions all over the world. It is not a Buddhist practice per se, or even a religious practice, and has existed for centuries. The only reason you and I ought to practice meditation is because our friend Sid used it as a tool to discover his innate wisdom, and lived happily ever after as a result. We too can touch the wisdom behind our confusion. We too can look at the display on our movie screen, and see it as illusory.

Sid is most commonly known for an act referred to as reaching enlightenment. What he discovered has been debated by countless people and described in numerous volumes of writing. For our purposes, we can just say that he awoke to reality as it is. Through the practice of meditation, he was able to find the ultimate calm: the calm of not always buying into whatever was on the movie screen of his mind. Instead he was able to turn his awareness to his own wisdom, often referred to as buddha nature, or basic goodness.

Each of us has the potential to be a buddha. We too possess the innate goodness that the Buddha discovered. Sid developed profound confidence in his own basic goodness, and from there he offered that goodness constantly. That's not a bad example of how shamatha can help schmucks like you and me.

You may not have ultimate enlightenment as your goal right now. That's cool. Really. However, if you want to open your heart more fully, learn to work with strong emotions that keep coming up, or just cut down on stress, you can use shamatha as a tool to loosen the addiction to buying into that never-ending display of our mind.

Here's an illustration of how it works. If you're at home, go fill up a glass of water. If you're not, just use your imagination for a moment. That crystal clear water is akin to our natural state. It is brilliant and without a ripple on it.

Now if you drop some dirt into your glass of water, things start to get messy. Particularly if you take a spoon and stir that dirt up. Try it!

This dirt tornado is symbolic of how we treat our mind on a daily basis. When a strong thought or emotion comes up, we spin it out into a thousand different scenarios. One clot of dirt might be "What did Laura mean by that weird e-mail?" and the mess of dirt around it the twelve different scenarios about what she's thinking, how we will respond, who to tell about it, and so on. When we spend our mental energy stirring up these "what-ifs," our mind is getting muddied.

OK, now stop stirring. Watch as the dirt settles to the bottom. While the dirt has dropped away, the water at the top returns to its natural clean and clear state.

In the same way, our mind is a backdrop for these strong emotions and feelings to play out. But no matter what, our mind is still innately vibrant and brilliant. It is basically good. When we don't get hooked by our cyclical display of thoughts, feelings, and emotions, we discover that being present with our innate wisdom is refreshing.

## MEDITATION ADVICE

Here's some advice on how to start putting down our pro-verbial stirring spoon, and start touching our basic goodness.

### LOCATION, LOCATION, LOCATION

You need to choose a place in your home to meditate. It's important to find a consistent, comfortable, quiet, and clean location. If you can't find a spot that has all four qualities, try to find a space that has at least a couple of them. Some people buy meditation cushions from local shops, while others prefer to throw a pillow or couch cushion on top of a blanket on the floor. If you have back problems, you might want to consider using a chair instead.

Place whatever setup works for you in a place that feels uplifted and spacious. It's not essential to find a place that is soundproof, but the idea is that you should be attracted to that space and you should be able to sit there for a period of time without being distracted. Don't sit facing your computer or TV, even if they're off. Your wall or a window should probably be OK.

### BODY

Take your seat on the cushion or chair. If you are sitting on a cushion, sit with your legs loosely crossed. If you're in a chair, place both feet firmly on the ground. You want to feel balanced and grounded when you sit down to meditate.

From this strong base, you can sit up straight (just like your mother always told you to). If it's a helpful image to reflect on, imagine a string at the top of your head pulling you straight up, elongating the spine. Don't force your body to do anything, but instead allow for your natural curvature. Relax your arms and shoulders.

The Buddha once had a student who was a musician, and who was particularly rigid when it came to his meditation practice. Our friend Sid said, "Remind me how you tune your instrument again. How should the strings be?"

The musician replied, "Not too tight and not too loose."

Sid said, "Yes. Meditate like that."

When you take your meditation posture, remember his advice. Don't tighten your muscles into knots, and don't slouch over like you're ready to go to sleep. Find your own middle way.

Rest your hands at your side. Then without moving your upper arms, bend your arms at the elbows and lift your hands up. Drop your hands palms down on your thighs. This will likely be a comfortable spot to rest them.

With your head resting gently on the top of your spine, slightly tuck in your chin. Relax the muscles in your face around your eyes, nose, and jaw. This might mean your mouth rests open, which is great. If it's helpful, you can rest your tongue up against the roof of your mouth.

One last thing about your posture: keep your eyes open. There are some schools of meditation that encourage you to close your eyes, while others say leave them open. I fall into the latter school. If the goal of our meditation practice is to remain present, it's a heck of a lot easier to do that if we're not purposefully tuning out one of our senses. Plus it's not uncommon for people to fall asleep during meditation. So try keeping your eyes open, resting your gaze in a loose and unfocused fashion somewhere around two to four feet ahead of you on the ground.

## BREATH

The object of our meditation practice is our breath. For one thing, we don't have to force the breath; it comes naturally, so it's easy to tune in to. Also, the breath's steadiness is soothing to the mind. The breath is also now. The breath is always now. And because the breath is always fresh, it's an excellent anchor to keep us rooted in the present moment.

Turn your attention to the physical sensation of both your out-breath and your in-breath. Don't change or manufacture your breathing at all, just let it happen as it always does.

## MIND

Inevitably you will get distracted from your breath. Some suddenly pressing issue pops into your mind, and you either want to jump off the meditation cushion to fix it, or figure it out on the spot. You might also find that you're replaying a phone conversation you had twenty minutes prior, or rehearsing what you're going to tell your date about yourself the next day.

Don't worry; every meditator in the history of meditation practice has had this exact same issue. I have no doubt that Sid in his "Where did all these thoughts come from?" stage also wondered what he was going to eat for dinner.

The thing to do when you find yourself lost in thought, emotion, or fantasy is to come back to the breath. If it is helpful, you can say "thinking" to yourself as a reminder that you are indeed thinking. You are not saying that your thought is good or bad, but you are just reminding yourself that what you really ought to be doing is returning your focus to the breath.

Have some faith that if the thought really is so incredibly good, it will still exist in some form after your meditation session. The poet Allen Ginsberg used to keep a journal by his meditation cushion. Brilliant thoughts would jump into his head, and his teacher Chögyam Trungpa Rinpoche (the meditation master who brought Shambhala Buddhism to the West) would call him out on it. Instead of saying, "Sure, write the next *Howl* here and now," Trungpa Rinpoche would say, "No. Put it down. Go back to the breath."

Whenever something seemingly important comes up in my mind during meditation, I reflect on that story and then definitively come back to focusing my attention on my breath. No matter what, come back. No leaping off the cushion allowed.

## TIMING

The most important thing is to keep your meditation sessions short and regular. Determine how long you plan to sit before getting down to it. Even if you can only fit in ten minutes a day, do that and stick with it.

Meditation practice is a bit like learning a new musical instrument. If you pick up the guitar once a month and play it for an hour or two, you slowly learn a few things, but you might end up discouraged when you can't play a full song in a year. But if you picked up that guitar for ten minutes a day, you would learn a few chords well, then a few basic songs, and in no time at all you would end up in a garage band.

The same idea applies to meditation. If you sit for an hour or two a month, it may not have much of an effect on you. However, if you sit for ten minutes a day, then over time you will get accustomed to meditation and see its effects start to permeate the rest of your life.

Meditation practice breeds mindfulness, which is quite simply paying attention to what is going on. We begin by seeing what is going on with the wild display on the movie screen that is our mind. We notice it, and we use shamatha to cut through our tendency to get drawn into every plot twist.

As we start to stabilize our mind, we notice that our meditation practice is becoming more enjoyable. We can have a sense of humor about the display on the screen. What previously was all drama is now a comedy. It's not that the plot is particularly different; we still see the impulse to get mad at someone or to play out how our next date could go. It's just that we are no longer powerless to turn our attention elsewhere. We can now turn our attention to getting in touch with our basic goodness. We can laugh at the display of our mind and not take it so seriously.

When we hit this point, we begin to have faith in our meditation practice because we are already benefiting from it. We are already in touch with our basic goodness, and we can begin to see goodness in the world around us.

# 3 / MANIFESTING THE QUALITIES OF THE TIGER

Growing up in the eighties, I used to love the cartoon *Super Friends*. It was a mix of all the coolest superheroes, including Superman, Batman, and Wonder Woman. The combined might of these characters continuously won out over any evil that they encountered.

In traditional Tibetan Buddhism, we have our own group of Super Friends. These are four mythical and nonmythical animals that represent different aspects of our training in wisdom and compassion. Individually they are the tiger, snow lion, *garuda* (part bird, part man), and dragon, and together they are known as the four dignities of Shambhala. When we consider them together, they are quite powerful. Instead of calling them forth with a cry or secret rings, we actually train in embodying the qualities of these animals and thus can manifest them on the spot.

Throughout the course of this book we will explore these four dignities of Shambhala. The qualities of these dignities are incredibly practical. We can look to these beings not as something otherworldly or esoteric but as examples of what we would like to embody in our own life. In studying the dignities we are discovering simple tools that help us contact our own basic goodness and manifest it in ways that are beneficial to ourselves and others.

Each dignity can be closely linked to one of the traditional paths of Tibetan Buddhism. As we explore each animal we

will progress along the three yanas, or vehicles, of the traditional Buddhist framework.

## THE TIGER AND THE HINAYANA PATH

The tiger is the first of these four animals. Many of the qualities of the tiger are traditionally referred to as part of the
Hinayana path. It is a path of focusing on one's own journey
to enlightenment, but does not preclude being of benefit to
others.

*Hinayana* is a funny word in that it directly translates to
"narrow, or lesser, vehicle." Some Buddhist traditions focus
solely on this path, and not surprisingly they take offense at
this translation. Instead of getting hung up on translations,
we can refer to the Hinayana as a process of getting your act
together. In other words, the Hinayana is a path of working
with our mind in a consistent way so that we manifest brilliant awakening.

I think that is something we can all get behind. The reason the image of the tiger is closely linked to the Hinayana
tradition is because the tiger is all about working with his
immediate environment with mindfulness, and thus waking up to his own life.

## THE THREE QUALITIES OF THE TIGER

There are three primary qualities that the tiger embodies:
discernment, gentleness, and precision.

### DISCERNMENT

The tiger carefully yet gracefully walks through the jungle.
He takes his time and observes his surroundings and then
acts based on that knowledge. In other words, the tiger
looks before he leaps.

For us twenty-first-century meditators, this might mean
looking at a shot of tequila and asking ourselves before we
take a sip, "Will this bring me happiness or will this bring

me pain?" Taking an honest look at our life, we might see that we are only drinking because we recently got dumped by our lover and want to cover up our pain. If that's the case, then we ought to realize that tequila is only a temporary Band-Aid; we'll sober up, and that person still won't be around. In this scenario, invoking the discernment of the tiger leads us to realize that getting drunk is not a viable route forward. Instead we need to deal with our pain directly, without self-medication.

By simply reflecting on our daily activities in this way, we learn our habitual patterns intimately. We learn that we drink when we're upset, we bite our nails when we're nervous, or we have sex when we're lonely. We take our mindfulness off the meditation cushion, and apply it to the nitty-gritty details of our life. Once we learn what aspects of our life we want to partake in more, and which we want .to nix, we have a route forward toward our own happiness.

## GENTLENESS

Often tigers are portrayed as violent beasts. However, if you have ever seen a female tiger with her cubs, she is incredibly gentle. The majesty of the tiger comes from the fact that while she is capable of slashing with her claws, more often than not she chooses not to.

The late Buddhist master Tulku Urgyen Rinpoche often said, "Being aggressive, you can accomplish some things, but with gentleness, you can accomplish all things." If you realize you're giving in to some habits that don't lead you toward happiness, you shouldn't berate yourself: "You jerk! You knew tequila would lead to a drunk dial, and now you've not only blown your shot at getting back together with her, but she's pissed!" That kind of inner dialogue is counterproductive.

The path of self-reflection is a long and turbulent one. If you get mad at yourself every time you miss a meditation session or drunk dial an ex, you may get disheartened and want to jump on some other path. That's why it's important to be gentle with yourself. The heart of the tiger's practice is that he is friendly to himself and kind with others.

Pema Chödrön, a teacher in the Shambhala Buddhist tradition, once encountered a gentleman who took this teaching as the root of his meditation journey. While giving a talk in Texas in the seventies, she looked out at the audience full of big men in ten-gallon hats and thought, "I don't know if what I said reached anyone here."

She was surprised years later when a gentleman introduced himself at one of her book signings as a participant in that Texas meditation program. He said that he had been meditating ever since her talk, and he had started off being very hard on himself. He would get very frustrated when he would catch himself in some fantasy and would yell "Thinking!" to himself. After contemplating her instruction, though, he decided to take a new approach, and instead found great joy in bringing himself back to the breath by gently saying, "Thinking, good buddy."

We all need to take a "good buddy" approach to our meditation practice if we want to see it flourish. Similarly, when we get frustrated at other aspects of our life, we need to cultivate a gentle approach. We can't beat ourselves up over everything. In twenty-six hundred years of meditation and teaching, no Buddhist master has ever said, "Frankly, you should just be a prick to yourself. That's how you create inner change."

Learning to walk gently through our world like the tiger is a practice. It takes reflection, learning, and patience. Ultimately we can embody this quality. Once we are gentle with ourselves, then we can offer that gentleness to others.

## PRECISION

As the tiger moves slowly through the jungle, he places each paw with incredible care. His senses are attuned to the world around him. In other words, he is present and awake to his daily environment.

All too often we rush through our life without any real

appreciation for what's going on right now. Through meditation practice, we learn to rest with our current situation: the physical sensation of our stiff back, our body breathing naturally, and the thoughts flowing through our mind. In our postmeditation world, we can be present with every aspect of our life, be it our work, school, our difficult family member on the telephone, or playing with our pets.

Sounds overwhelming to always be present? Try starting with something very simple: washing the dishes. Right now, go walk over to your kitchen sink. If there's no dish there, feel free to make yourself a snack first.

Now pick up the dish. Feel its weight in your hands. Turn on the water. Feel the heat of the water on your skin. Take your sponge, and feel how its texture changes as it goes from dry and brittle to wet and soft. Wash your dish carefully, and when you are done, admire the beauty of a clean plate.

Be present for simple acts like this, and you may be surprised how content you end up.

Training in being present with various aspects of our life leads to a sense of slowing down and gaining precision. If you have ever stopped in the midst of a busy city street, you know the sense of cutting through the speed that surrounds us like a knife. We don't have to clog the sidewalks to gain that feeling. We can be present during a colleague's boring work presentation, or with our spouse when we are making love. We appreciate what it takes to do well at our job or to be a good boyfriend or girlfriend, because we cut through the speed that surrounds us.

When we cut through our habitual speed, we may find we are taking the same care with aspects of our life as the tiger does when he hunts. We can survey our closet in the morning just as the tiger surveys his landscape. As he carefully chooses his prey, we too can slow down and carefully choose what we wish to wear. As the tiger catches his prey with deft movements, we bring the same sense of precision to the way we tie our tie or arrange our scarf. That precision looks and feels very good. We are embodying the majesty of the tiger through being present and focusing on being precise.

It takes great bravery to take an honest look at our life and say, "I want to make a change." It takes specific know-how to make that change. Through studying the four dignities, we can learn about and embody their qualities. We can call forth the qualities of these Super Friends, for they already exist within us. In the case of the tiger, we can manifest discernment, gentleness, and precision in a wide range of our activities. These qualities are the tools for change and in the next three chapters we will explore them in greater depth.

In Tibetan, there is a word for the warrior who is willing to undergo this internal transformation in order to be of service to the world: *pawo*, "one who is brave." The bravery is not in struggling with our world, but in taking this honest look at our life. Following the path of the tiger, snow lion, garuda, and dragon, we have the potential to fully realize who we are, and from there offer our genuineness to the world.

# 4 / DISCERNING YOUR OWN MANDALA

The purpose of studying Buddhism is not to study Buddhism, but to study ourselves.

—*Shunryu Suzuki Roshi*

In the opening scene of the 2001 film *Ocean's Eleven,* our protagonist, Danny Ocean, is about to be released from a New Jersey prison. He confidently struts out of the penitentiary wearing a tuxedo with a bow tie loosely hanging from his neck, and within a matter of a few weeks he has pulled off a heist that lands him eleven million dollars and the love of his ex-wife.

Here is the part that was spliced and left on the cutting-room floor: Danny was in jail for four years preparing single-mindedly for those few weeks after his release. What appears casual and nonchalant to the viewer is a scrupulously planned-out chain of events, laid out by someone who had turned his whole being to making his goal a reality. He had a certain motivation set in his mind, and as soon as he could he pursued it precisely. The Indian pandit Shantideva once said:

Herons, cats, and burglars
Achieve what they intend
By going silently and unobserved.
Such is the constant practice of a sage.

Shantideva here uses the term *sage* when he references a common Buddhist term: *bodhisattva*. This term can also be translated from Sanskrit as "openhearted warrior" or "open-minded warrior." A warrior in this case is not someone who looks for fights, but as we discussed earlier, someone who is willing to engage and confront their habitual way of relating to the world. Whereas the thief is motivated by money and success, the bodhisattva is motivated by working with their own mind in order to benefit others.

Buddhism is often perceived as a moralistic religion. When I was in college, I would tell people that I was a Buddhist, and they would balk at the beer in my hand and the hot girl on my arm. They assumed that Buddhists aren't supposed to drink or have sex. But Buddhism is not some super-religion that is more puritanical than other religious traditions. Just as in other spiritual traditions, there are some Buddhists who choose to live a life of abstinence and others who do not. In fact, many Buddhist practitioners are wonderful drinkers and lovers.

There is some fine print, though. Buddhism informs us that we should be familiar with the intention behind our actions, and whether what we do will have a positive or negative effect on those around us. The Indian meditation master Atisha wrote, "All activities should be done with one intention." That intention is a willingness to be kind to ourselves, and thus influence the world around us in a positive way.

The individual who wishes to embody the qualities of the tiger turns their discernment to their own life. After engaging our mind for some time in meditation, we begin to understand what it is that drives us to do certain things. Getting back together with an ex may not have much to do with giving them another chance, but more to do with not wanting to feel lonely anymore. Switching careers may be a way to breathe fresh air into our daily routine, but it could also be an escape from a difficult boss. When we can catch ourselves about to step into painful or pleasurable situations, we can reflect on our motivation.

While not a Buddhist, Hamlet really grasped these teachings on knowing our intention. As he eloquently told Horatio, "There is nothing good or bad but thinking makes it so." A beer by itself is not a bad thing. In fact, when our intention is to relax with some friends and catch up, a beer is often a great motivator to get together. Alternatively, when we are angry and our motivation is to forget a botched presentation at work, drinking serves as merely an escape from reality. In either case, we can't blame the beer when we wake up with an awful hangover. The beer didn't make us do anything: it was our own mind not being able to grasp our intention that put us in such a state.

Often people like to practice meditation in the morning before going about their daily routine. It can be quite a gift to oneself to take an extra ten or twenty minutes for self-reflection before rushing into the daily grind. As we sit down to meditate in the morning, various versions of "What is super-important today?" come up. We can use this opportunity to continuously return to the present moment instead of getting caught up in the torrent of thoughts. We can connect with our motivation, whether it is to slog through our day and not get into a fight with our coworker, help a friend through a difficult breakup, or if we can muster it, to try to live our day with mindfulness and discernment.

In both Hinduism and Buddhism, the term *mandala* in its most generic sense is a sort of organizational chart. Often within Buddhism, the mandala is used as a tool to represent a certain lineage figure or deity that one might meditate on. That deity is at the center of the mandala, and then a secondary circle surrounds it, which contains the deity's crew. Surrounding that is another layer of beings, then another, and so on, until all sentient beings are represented.

Such mandalas are symbolic of the mandala you create for yourself without even realizing it. Whatever you take as your chief motivation is at the center. Let's say it is a sense of protecting yourself from ever feeling upset. If you build your mandala with the notion of protecting yourself at the core, then in the next layer around that, you would develop habitual patterns that shield you from harmful activities. For example, you wouldn't try new things or meet new people.

Outside that thick wall of the mandala is another circle that likely includes people already in your life who always tell you nice things and make you feel good about yourself. Then the layer outside that could be all the nice places where you always go, and the item on the menu you always order so you will never have to be disappointed by change. You can create layer after layer in order to build your whole identity and lifestyle around self-preservation.

I would say a good number of the people in America take "getting ahead in life" as the center of their personal mandala. That can manifest as making their life revolve around their career, getting the perfect spouse, or finding ways to get rich quick. Through trial and error, these same people often end up disappointed and seeking something else. Either they could not attain their goal and they feel burned-out, or they have attained their goal and they already hunger for something new.

Imagine a world where everyone instead took a motivation like being generous and made that the center of their mandala. With generosity as your core, the next layer might be skillful ideas on how to best give your time, energy, and money to the local community. The next layer might be people who would encourage this behavior or recipients of your generosity, and so on until you find that your whole life has been influenced by the structure of this mandala, and you are genuinely a generous person.

To return to our friend Danny Ocean, he had placed at the center of his mandala a certain level of covetousness: pulling a heist so ingenious that it would win his ex-wife back. So the center of Danny Ocean's mandala was gaining things for himself. To that end, Danny built an elaborate mandala of colleagues, diversions, and cons around that motivation. He lured people into his mandala with the promise of money, and ultimately his single-pointedness of intention and years of contemplation won out.

In contrast, my friend David left his job a few years back to start an environmental consulting company. He felt so strongly that the biggest issue of our generation would be global warming that he took a strong resolve to educate people on environmental issues. He struggled through financial hardships, disappointing meetings with publicists and investors, and yet he never forgot his motivation of trying to be of benefit to Mother Earth.

The motivation to raise awareness of the Green movement was at the center of his mandala, influencing his daily behavior and supporting him to the point that he is now able to see the effects of his work on others. While the work may not always look like he originally imagined it, he has had a profound influence on hundreds if not thousands of people, who are now doing little things each day to reduce their carbon footprint. His strong motivation to raise awareness of environmental issues has not only made his life one he deems to be of value, but has also infected other people with the bug of motivation to educate and take action on environmental issues.

The interesting thing that Danny Ocean and my friend David have in common is that they had an effect on those around them, while never aggressively forcing their ideas onto people. Having a core motivation you believe in breeds a sense of ease and skill around working with others. You let your motivation shine, and other people are attracted to your passion and commitment.

For some people, discerning their motivation might lead to major life changes. You may realize one day that all you want to do is breed pit bulls, and you decide that this intention will guide your life for a period of time. That would likely cause some changes around the house. However, if that brought you a sense of contentment, you could live a long life dedicated to the welfare of pit bulls. The point is that you waded through the muck of your mind to discern a path that you felt confident about.

A friend of mine went to a meditation program and decided that she would spend the rest of her life involved in spiritual endeavors, never again taking on a worldly job. Most people would say, "Aha! That's a bit nobler than looking after dogs!" In my opinion there is nothing inherently good or bad about either situation "but thinking makes it so."

When my spiritual teachers are approached by students with questions about major life decisions, I am often surprised by their responses. Over and over again I have heard them say that what makes our life spiritual or worldly is not our vocation, but our view. For example, if the view of my friend who wants to enter the nunnery is to hide out and never work again, then that may not be such a good thing. That would be anti-bodhisattva; it would be closing down and hiding from her life. If her view is to cultivate sanity and compassion within herself in order to share that with others, then perhaps she ought to give it a try. It is her view in making this decision that is important.

For many of us, we are not in the position to up and leave our daily grind. We need to maintain our 9 to 5 job, and can barely find time to squeeze in ten to twenty minutes of meditation a day. However, with the right view and the right intention, we can use our existent daily routine as a framework to live a spiritually fulfilling life.

Discerning and following through on our motivation is easier said than done. While we may wish to bring our awareness to the things that are important to us, we often get distracted. Our ability to pay attention is weak, and we can go a full day without cultivating whatever it is we want to keep at the center of our mandala. However, remembering our motivation and coming back to it over and over again is just as valuable a meditation as shamatha. Throughout our day, instead of coming back to the breath, we can continuously come back to what it is we want to do with our life. Whether we are trying to rob a casino or raise awareness about global warming, as long as we hold true to our root motivation we are still on a journey.

A few years ago, the notions of the thief and the bodhi-sattva collided for me. I was exiting Grand Central Terminal in New York City when I found that the taxi stand had been moved to a different location due to construction. A gentleman approached me and offered to lead me to the cab stand, saying that he was a dispatcher and could help me get a taxi to the airport.

Hailing a cab, he asked for a flat fare to the airport. The amount seemed a bit excessive, but since I was in a hurry I handed it over. He leaned in and spoke to the driver, appearing to hand the money to the driver while I got into the cab. As soon as the door closed, he ran off. I inquired as to whether money had changed hands, and it turned out it had not. I had been scammed. I threw open the car door and ran after the man, but he had already disappeared.

Over the next few hours on my plane ride cross-country, I had a lot of time to think about the experience. I started by feeling sorry for myself. I was just out of college and didn't have much money. Then I began to get mad at the man. Who was he to take my money? Then I began to think about all the various motivations someone could have for scamming others. The man could have been a junkie looking for money for his latest fix. I fixated on that possibility for a while. Alternatively he could have been out of work with no leads on a job and kids to feed.

I realized that I would never know why he did what he did. I could only hope that his intention was to use the money in a way that benefited others as well as him. I came to realize that he gave me an opportunity to contemplate the life of someone who was likely not as fortunate as I am. I gave thanks for what I had, and came to understand that he had helped me return to my root motivation: trying to help others. Having contemplated the occurrence many times since then and having learned a lot about myself from the experience, I cannot help wondering if the man was a thief or a bodhisattva in disguise.

As you begin to discern what aspects of your life you

want to cultivate and which you need to cut out, you learn a great deal about yourself. You can then begin to consider how you want to turn your mind. Do you want to turn it to your career? Do you want to turn it to living a life based on compassion? Do you want to turn it to compassionately engaging your existent career? Why is this activity important to you? Do you want to leave your job in order to focus on raising a child? Do you want to enter a monastic path? Do you want to spend more time caring for your aging grandmother?

Through becoming inquisitive about our life, we can discern how we want to move forward. We can take our root motivation and make it central to who we are. From there we radiate out. All our activities can be infused with our core belief. When we do that, we live a life we can be proud of, and a life that has a positive effect on everyone we encounter.

# 5 / BEING GENTLE WITH YOUR INCREDIBLE HULK SYNDROME

After we have been meditating for a little while, we may begin to see some gaps in the midst of our waterfall of thoughts. We begin to realize that our mind is fundamentally open, clear, and neutral. But as refreshing as such experiences are, those glimpses into our basic state don't happen that often when we're brand-new meditators. What does come up a great deal is a series of strong emotions.

The interesting thing about emotions is that, like all thoughts, they are not considered good or bad for our meditation practice. They are merely the energetic display of our mind. They are thoughts with a lot of energy behind them. When we sit down to meditate, we might be thinking of our upcoming birthday bash, making a mental checklist for our Monday morning, indulging in wild fantasies about the barista at our favorite espresso bar, or feeling drowsy because we got in at two a.m. the night before. As with all forms of thoughts, we acknowledge them gently, recognize them as something other than what we're supposed to be doing, and turn our attention back to the breath.

Then along comes a strong emotion. These are harder to navigate away from because they feel so incredibly real. It is as if they have a physical presence in our body. When we feel anger, that thought makes our stomach churn and our muscles tighten. When we feel love, there's a certain lightness to our being. My favorite example of strong emotion is heartbreak because it's so true to its name: when we experience heartbreak, we literally feel like our heart is breaking in two. These are not easy things to label "thinking" and turn away from.

The first thing to remember is that these emotions are not your enemy. They are fluid and open experiences. They are the dirt swirling in a glass of water before it settles to the bottom. Like the dirt in the glass, your emotions won't always be active on the surface unless you keep stirring them up. In other words, it's not your strong emotions that get you in trouble, it's the fact that you get hooked by them.

Sometimes people mistake the term *enlightenment* to mean some robot-like state where you are unable to feel emotions. The great meditation masters I have experienced are anything but robots. They feel emotions a great deal, but they do not get fixated on them. They can feel great love or loss, but will not get hooked by the emotion to the point where it consumes them. They have learned to put the stirring spoon down.

Most of us have barely looked at our emotional state in depth, and we get hooked very easily when something like anger comes up. Take the Incredible Hulk, for example. Comic-book character Bruce Banner was a mild-mannered scientist, but when he got angry enough, he would turn into a giant, raging, green monster. Bruce would be going about his day and then stub his toe, which was his personal final straw that day, and suddenly he would grow huge, rip his clothes off, and tear down his kitchen.

That's a level of giving in to emotion that causes a great deal of harm. However, if Bruce had learned to stop for a moment, feel the mild pain caused by hurting his toe but not get sucked into an angry cycle, thinking about all his troubles, then he probably wouldn't have had to keep losing the deposits on his apartments.

## KLESHAS

There's a Tibetan word for Incredible Hulk syndrome, which is *klesha*. *Klesha* can best be translated as "afflictive emotion." It is the sense that when a strong emotion gets its hooks in you, your mind spins out of control. Traditionally there are five main ways that kleshas are said to manifest. They are a stuck sense of:

1. Passion or attachment
2. Aggression
3. Ignorance or prejudice
4. Pride
5. Jealousy

We have all had experiences of those five emotions, and we know how painful it can be when they get their hooks into us. It can be paralyzing if we can't think of anything else but them.

Sometimes we might experience all five of these stuck emotions simultaneously. When you receive a text message telling you that your date for the night doesn't have time to get together, you might experience a whole whirlwind of emotions. You might think, "I wanted to try this out but I'm feeling rejected, so fuck him. He's stupid, I'm awesome. But I just don't want him to ever date anyone but me."

Let's analyze that display of Incredible Hulk syndrome, or klesha. Up until that moment you were stuck in lusting after this guy. Then you got a text message, and your mind revved up. Instead of catching yourself at that moment before the madness began, you gave in to the worst-case scenario: "It's because of me." You felt rejected, and that led you into anger: "Fuck him." Then in order to ease that pain, you jumped over to another form of klesha, namely prejudice: "He's stupid." You had to protect your vanity, so you made a leap over to pride: "I'm awesome." You rounded out the whole thing with jealousy, as if you were trying to collect the complete klesha

set: "But I just don't want him to ever date anyone but me."
By that point you're giant and green and kicking over trees.

If you had caught yourself before entering that vicious spiral, you would have been able to respond in a kinder way to that individual, thus salvaging the potential for future interactions or dates. It's not impossible to do. The basic training in catching yourself before getting hooked by afflictive emotions is—surprise, surprise—meditation practice.

When we're on the meditation cushion and a strong emotion rears its head, the first thing to do is remember what we're doing: we're learning to be present with our emotional display, and not get stuck by it. If you're thinking about how angry you are that your boss has been keeping you late at work day after day, then try coming back to the breath. See if that works. Notice if that emotion comes up again, and if so, if it's stronger. Try to drop the story line around why she keeps you late, and just feel the underlying emotion.

Because we're so used to being led around by our emotions, it may become harder and harder to come back to our present experience. In that case, take one minute to use the practice of contemplation to look at the situation. Think to yourself, "Why am I mad about my boss keeping me late? She's not even here! I'm not even at work! That's not what I want to focus on right now." Then try returning your attention to the breath.

Maybe that doesn't work for you. If that's the case, then pause your meditation practice and try looking for the physical location of your anger. It's important not to get swept up in analysis of every ache in your body. Just set a certain amount of time, five minutes maybe, and at the end of those five minutes return to shamatha practice.

During those five minutes, though, try to identify where in your body your anger resides. Is it in your arm muscles? The pit of your stomach? Your head? Is it solid or fluid? Does it have a color? A shape? This form of analysis might help you realize that the emotion is not as stuck and solid as it initially felt.

If none of the above helps you, then it may not be the best time to meditate. Instead, do something that will relax your body and, as a result, your mind. You can take a hot shower, go for a walk, or drink a warm cup of tea. Then once you feel more grounded, try going back to the cushion to meditate. My root teacher, Sakyong Mipham Rinpoche, is the head of the Shambhala Buddhist lineage. He often says, "Knowing when we can meditate is honest meditation." Applying the correct skillful method in order to work with your emotional upheaval is synonymous with applying the gentleness of the tiger.

Through meditation practice, we are working with the energy of the emotion as a transformative experience. We are getting to know our emotions. We should not immediately hop off the cushion anytime we feel like our meditation practice is getting too intense, and go and act on our emotion. At the same time, we don't need to outright reject our emotions and consider them some negative aspect of our mind. Resting gently with our emotional state is the middle way between those two extremes. Continuing to stay with the energy of our emotions is how we learn to see them as reflections of our mind.

## RENUNCIATION

While the meditation cushion is a prime training ground for learning about our emotional states, it is important to reflect on how our emotions affect us during the twenty-three-plus hours of our day when we are not meditating. We are so used to acting on whatever emotion springs to our mind. This means we are capable of being quick with a joke that does not land, or with a retort if we feel threatened. More often than not, we cause harm when we let our emotions lead us around like a big dog on a leash.

Thankfully, not unlike a misbehaving dog, we can put our foot down and say "No." We can engage in renunciation.

Applying the gentleness of the tiger, we can notice when an impulse arises, and practice kindness by not immediately acting on it. We can take the same gap we experience in our meditation practice, and come back to the present moment. So if we see a new outfit that we can't afford, the sensible thing is not to act on our longing for it. If we do, then our bank account ends up overdrawn, our friends have to pay for our dinner, and we're all unhappy in the long run.

Renunciation is a principle in Buddhism that is often misunderstood. It is not the idea that we are giving up every pleasurable aspect of our life so we can live a stale and boring existence. It's the sense that when we apply the tiger's discernment to our life, we see which aspects we want to cultivate and which we want to reject. From there, we can gently extricate the aspects of our life that we realize are causing us harm.

When we run into someone who really angers us, renunciation means we have learned that giving in to emotional flare-ups only adds tension into our relationship. Instead, we cut that potential emotional hook, and greet them with kindness, or if that's not possible, walk away from the oncoming outburst. In either case, we are acknowledging our emotional state while not getting hooked to the point where we are causing harm.

The ability to stay with our strong emotions is a direct result of our training in the tiger's gentleness. On the outer level, you do not allow the emotion to take over, which is a kindness to yourself and to those with whom you interact. Granted, this is at best a temporary solution; the emotion is sure to arise again. That is why on the inner level, we work on developing a relationship with emotional patterns through the gentleness of the practice of meditation.

Through applying the quality of being friendly to yourself, you learn to not reject your present experience. You can stay present, and learn from the emotion. Over time your ability to stay present changes how you relate to emotions.

You don't have to fear them or be trapped by them, but you can instead stay with their underlying energy so you are not at war with yourself.

## Writing Exercise for Working with Emotions

In the past, when I have been faced with a strong emotion that has gotten its hooks into me, this contemplation has proven particularly helpful.

1. Meditate for ten minutes and be aware of what comes up.
2. After you stop meditating, identify the primary emotional experience that came up during meditation. It can be a recent scenario that brought up strong emotions, or perhaps something further back in your past.
3. Sit down and write about the situation. Describe how it makes you feel. Don't just say "upset," "nervous," or "annoyed," but actually go in depth, and describe the qualities of the emotion you are feeling. Really look at it and explore it.
4. Put your pen down and turn your attention to your body. How does your body feel right now? Is the emotion present? If so, where does it reside in your body? Can you stay with this feeling, or is it too painful?
5. Write a bit about how the emotion feels right now. Remain gentle but inquisitive in examining the difference between the experience of the emotion during meditation and afterward.
6. Return to the cushion and sit for another five to ten minutes. See if the emotion comes up again, and try the techniques mentioned earlier in this chapter to further examine it.

No matter what comes of this writing exercise, remember to remain gentle with yourself.

If we are meditating regularly and doing our best to work with our emotions, but we still feel like we are struggling with them and getting hooked by them, we need to remain patient and remember that inner change does not happen overnight. Through gently examining our emotional state, we learn valuable lessons about how we get trapped in the Incredible Hulk syndrome, and about what allows us to carefully avoid those traps in the future.

# 6 / THIS MOMENT IS THE OCCASION

In practicing meditation, we're not trying to live up to some kind of ideal—quite the opposite. We're just being with our experience, whatever it is.

—*Pema Chödrön*

Meditation is a process of self-discovery. The goal should not be trying to attain a state of perfection by adding anything on top of what we are. We are learning to be the perfect being we are already. We possess basic goodness, but we have wrapped ourselves up in so many layers of confusion and habitual patterns that it is hard to always remember that.

Those layers of confusion manifest as the million ways we shut down from our present experience and divide the world into "us" and "them." The moment we are faced with a long line at an airport, we think, "Who's in charge here? They ought to have known so many people were coming; people book their flights months in advance. How could they be so unprepared?" The key word in that statement is "they." You are right, "they" are wrong. The amorphous "they" is always in the wrong.

The thing is, when we get to the front of that line and there's a stressed-out airline employee who is just trying to get everyone on their flight, our heart softens. "They" is not amorphous anymore. It's this poor woman who is now being kind to us. When we turn our mind away from our annoyance and into the present, we see that other people suffer just as we do. Everyone is trying to make their flight. This woman is doing the best she can. The way to help out in a scenario like this is to just remain present with everyone concerned, and offer yourself as you are. Since you are basically good, you have a lot to offer.

The quality of precision that the tiger embodies plays a role here. As with other elements in following the tiger's example, we keep coming back to one key idea: being present with every detail in our life. We are always turning our mind to something, be it how ready we are for our lunch break, what sort of clothes we want to buy, or how much farther we have to go on a long jog. Let us turn our mind to whatever is going on right now.

Thus far, we have talked about formal meditation practice as a time when we turn our mind to the breath, and use it to anchor ourselves in the present moment. Sakyong Mipham Rinpoche often jokes that if we're not applying a sense of discipline during our formal meditation practice, we might as well just be sitting there waiting for the bus. In either case, we're spacing out; it's just the location that is different.

To invert that scenario, when we are sitting waiting for our bus, we could use that as an opportunity to sneak in a few minutes of shamatha meditation. While it may be louder than our meditation practice at home, this is a nice way to allow some time to feel grounded in the midst of a busy day.

Virtually anything in our daily routine can be a meditation practice, though. We don't need to pause whatever we are doing every five minutes to come back to our breath. We can mindfully do any of our routine activities. We can bring our mind to the fact that we are combing our hair and do that precisely, instead of just speeding through it lost in thought. We can take great care getting dressed in the morning and take pleasure in going through that process, instead of thinking about what we have to do later on in the day. At the end of the day, we can brush our teeth and do that simple task well, instead of running through the various events that took place earlier. When we tune in to our life, we might be surprised by how much contentment we feel. As Chögyam Trungpa Rinpoche once said:

> The way to experience nowness is to realize that this very moment, this very point in your life, is always the occasion. So the consideration of where you are and what you are, on the spot, is very important. That is one reason that your family situation, your domestic everyday life, is so important. You should regard your home as sacred, as a golden opportunity to experience nowness. Appreciating sacredness begins very simply by taking an interest in all the details of your life.

Applying the precision of the tiger can appear as taking pride in the most basic aspects of our life. Once in a while I enjoy a good steak. Specifically I enjoy going to the market, picking out the meat, taking it home, seasoning it, staying attuned to the steak as it cooks, letting it sit for a few moments afterward, and then eating it slowly. While cooking a meal is a pretty common occurrence for many of us, I think that I would not get the same satisfaction out of eating a steak if I had merely ordered it at a restaurant. Turning my mind to the precision and mindfulness of cooking the meal is what allows me to enjoy it so much.

If we allow the precision of the tiger to imbue the basic activities of our life, such as getting dressed in the morning or cooking dinner, then our attitude shifts. As Chögyam Trungpa Rinpoche wrote, we begin to treat our world as sacred. We are taking the ordinary and, through appreciating it, making it extraordinary. The "extra" comes from the simple fact that we are appreciating things as they are. We are imbuing the various parts of our day with a sense of the sacred merely by considering each activity worthy of our undivided attention.

Being present with cooking a good meal is an informal meditation practice, but still a good one. As with our formal shamatha practice, we are using it to cut through fixed mind. We are taking time off from the habitual loop of thoughts that play out in our mind. We are taking time off from always fixating on "me."

So much of our pain comes from looking at our life in a "me" versus "the world" mentality. We think we have to fight our way through our day, believing that if we don't make our presence felt, people will walk all over us. We spend so much of our day lost in thinking about what we need to do, because we are afraid of messing up. That can be an exhausting way to live.

We need to relax our assumptions and expectations. Treating our world as sacred is one way we can relax. It can be refreshing to take a break and just be present with the world around us, and experience the beauty of our life. We can be present with our daily commute, and enjoy seeing two children dancing on the subway. This experience perks us up. We don't have to make a big deal of chasing after the most exotic dance troupe in the world; we can appreciate the one right in front of us.

As we train in being precise and present, difficult situations may arise. Our life is not all steak and children dancing. It's also sickness, betrayal, and death. For most of us, the habitual response to seeing these aspects of our life is to shut down. We want to say, "Not for me. I'll turn my mind to other, more pleasant things until this situation resolves itself."

We all have our escapes. Some of us watch TV, some of us bite our nails, some of us do drugs. However, when we are done indulging in our escape plan, even if we think we did a really good job of covering over our difficult scenario, our pain is still there. It is waiting in the present moment for us to meet it.

This meditation thing we have been practicing is meant for this very scenario. It's a bit like when Rocky keeps trying to run up the steps of the Philadelphia Museum of Art. He trains and trains, and at one point in the movie you think, "Is this it? This is going on for a long time." Then he steps into the ring with Apollo Creed, and he has to face the reality of what he has been training for. That is when the movie gets juicy.

Our life is no different. When we sit for ten or twenty minutes a day, we are in training. We are running the steps of our mind. Lest we think our meditation practice is boring, some new big pain will come along and wake us up from our habitual routine. We might get a phone call in the middle of the night, and learn that our father has been rushed to the hospital due to a heart attack. At that point, we have to step into the ring with our pain. We have to face it head-on as warriors.

The funny thing is, the best way to deliver a knockout punch to the pain we feel is to do nothing. Instead of getting angry at the pain or turning our back to it, all we have to do is be present with what we are feeling. Our pain may deliver several jabs to our gut. We may feel like throwing up. However, if we can be present with our pain, it exhausts itself. It sags and falters and ultimately collapses. If we do not indulge our pain but instead just allow ourselves to feel it, we go through an intimate healing process. The pain washes over us like a wave, and we come out the other end unscathed and feeling better for it.

The warrior who embodies the tiger realizes that sometimes the kindest thing to do in a situation is to do nothing. When your father breaks down in tears because he is worried about dying, the compassionate thing may not be making a mental checklist of how he should adjust his diet to prevent another heart attack. Your father may just need to vent, and the truly kind thing to do is sit there and listen.

Listening is a lost art in our society. The tiger knows how to do it. He can lie still and listen to the sounds of the jungle for long stretches of time. Then, knowing the area well, he knows exactly when and how to pounce. We too can listen more deeply to the people we care about, and learn when it is appropriate to act, or not act, which might actually be the kinder option. Maybe you find yourself with someone as they have entered the dying process. At that point, you might want to run around and get the dying individual all sorts of magazines and entertainment so neither of you has to acknowledge the situation in a real way. That emotional cover-up often only makes the process harder. Instead you can learn from the example of the tiger, and not do anything but be present and precise with the individual. You can sit there and hold their hand. You can talk about their experience. You can offer yourself fully, as you are. That is genuine kindness.

Whether we are facing a pleasurable, painful, or even mundane situation, we can transform it into a sacred moment simply by being present. We do not always have to shut down or turn our back to the world. We can embrace it as the training ground of the warrior. Through being precise with our actions and training in the art of not having to fix everything, we get in touch with our basic goodness.

Confidence in our goodness shines forth like a light in a dark cave. This form of confidence in ourselves and in the sacredness of our world is the manifestation of our own perfection. This confidence was always there, but we are finally letting it shine.

# 7 / ATTENDING TO THE DETAILS OF YOUR LIFE

Thus far we have talked about relating to our mind on and off the cushion. But what about the practical applications of our discipline? How can the qualities of the tiger inform our 9 to 5 job, our home, our clothes, our money, our body, and our travel? Let's explore in depth the fundamental ways we can apply these teachings.

## OUR 9 TO 5

Almost everyone experiences a great deal of stress and pressure due to work or school. At times, pressure builds to a boiling point and someone snaps. The age-old Buddhist instruction for facing aggression in our lives is to give it a lot of space.

Imagine a bull in a pen at a rodeo. The bull is provoked and becomes angry. His reaction is to kick and buck about. The individual who then tries to ride on said bull has a very hard time working with the bull's rage. However, if you put that bull in a wide open field and leave him be, he would run about until he exhausted himself.

We are all like this bull. When your coworker or fellow student is angry, you have two choices. One is to get into it with them and see how long you can ride that bull before getting thrown off. The other is to give them lots of space to express themselves until they tire themselves out.

The warrior who embodies the gentleness of the tiger has faith in this discipline. That faith comes from experience. You can try it out for yourself and see if it works. If someone freaks out in front of you, you can say, "Uh-oh. You better watch out. If you keep pushing me, I'm going to get gentler with you. You really don't want to see me then!" This is the antithesis of buying into our version of the Incredible Hulk syndrome. The person can jump up and down and go into a rage, but you will simply outlast them. You have unlimited energy to face these difficult situations, so long as you don't bite the hook presented by strong emotions and refrain from reacting.

## OUR HOME

So many of us view our home as a hideout, a fortress of solitude where we can get away with not being mindful or kind. It's our escape. The path of meditation teaches us that there is no such thing as an escape. If we want to truly grow as human beings, we need to treat every environment we are in, including our home, as a training ground.

When starting off on the path of meditation, it is helpful to create an environment that encourages the quality of wakefulness in our being. There is a Tibetan term, *drala*, which can be translated as "energy above aggression." This energy is inherent in our being and in our surroundings. It is most present when we pay attention to what is going on around us. It is the energy we experience when we are not tuned in to our internal chatter and aggression, but instead tuned in to our environment.

Take a moment and think about how you feel when you wake up in the morning and your room is a mess. You get up to stumble to the bathroom, and as you are avoiding a pile of clothes, you trip over your laptop, kicking it across the room. You're already swearing at yourself, and you have only been awake for two minutes.

Now visualize waking up to a room that is spotless. You

walk carefree to the bathroom, look at yourself in a clean mirror, and smile. Drala is the energy that is produced when you have taken care of the details of your life so that everything has a certain radiance to it.

Just like the tiger, we can be precise with our environment, and as such we can experience the majesty of presiding over it. There are a thousand little things we can do to our home that will bring a sense of dignity to where we spend our time. Look around your bedroom. Not surprisingly, investing in framing pictures or art pieces adds new life to the space. You know that the room feels more spacious if your clothes are put away and your sheets are fitted on the bed instead of lying in a pile on the floor.

These are simple acts, but we often lack the discipline to do all of them. Turning our attention to our home and creating a sacred environment uplifts us and allows our mindfulness practice to flow smoothly.

## Our Clothes

Another way to magnetize drala energy is through the clothes we wear. Magazines today teach us that if you want to look good, you need to have a few thousand dollars you can pour into your wardrobe. That is not the case. If you see any of the great Tibetan teachers, they appear radiant even in very simple robes. This radiance that shines forth is known as *ziji* in the Tibetan tradition. *Ziji* can be translated as "brilliant confidence." The uplifted and dignified appearance of these teachers comes from confidence in their own basic goodness.

You can apply the qualities of the tiger so that you too appear radiant. The tiger surveys his landscape and chooses his activity carefully. You can survey your closet, see what you would like to buy, and go out and precisely shop for that item. You can bring discernment to your shopping and pick beautiful items that are affordable. You can consider the material and the craft of each garment. When we take this level of care, we feel good about the items we pick. We do not feel guilty, because we are not maxing out our credit cards or buying unnecessary items. We are bringing a sense of contentment into our life through completing a day of shopping with mindfulness.

As we get dressed, we can take pride in our appearance and dress for whatever occasion we face. We can take responsibility for our appearance, and shave, wax, and trim appropriately. We are no longer babies. Our mothers are not going to appear out of thin air to make sure we look good. It is up to us to take pride in how we present ourselves to the world.

When I go on solitary retreat, I always bring nice clothes. Even though no one will ever see me, I feel a sense of happiness from putting them on in the morning. When I see myself in the mirror, I am perked up by the cleanliness and vibrancy of the colors. You don't have to dress to impress other people. Instead try dressing to uplift yourself.

## Our Money

There is a common misunderstanding that as meditators we're not supposed to care about money. Our spirituality is one thing, and how we make our dough is another. That is not the case. If you think you can apply these teachings to only certain aspects of your life, you are missing the point. You have a responsibility to yourself to investigate your relationship to money.

I have met very few people who relate well to their money. So many of us will go to the ATM, take out some cash, and quickly throw away the receipt so we are not faced with the reality of our remaining balance. We then take the sum of money that we received and spend it without much awareness. Two days pass, and we wonder where a hundred dollars escaped to. This is a sign of an unhealthy relationship to money, and over time this behavior will cause us to become frustrated and self-critical.

You can cultivate a nonaggressive attitude toward your financial reality. You can stop ignoring how you feel about it, and apply the tiger's discernment, gentleness, and precision to your relationship with money.

The first step is to apply gentle curiosity and attention to your financial picture in order to see it more clearly. You can contemplate your intention for how you want to spend your money. From there, you apply the discernment of the tiger by determining what tendencies you want to cultivate and which you want to reject. You can take a look at your bank statement and draft a budget for yourself. Be gentle with yourself; if you spend too much one day, it's no cause for panic. Just learn from that experience and move on.

As we continue to explore our relationship with money, we develop more awareness and kindness to ourselves. We see that with a bit of effort, we can keep track of our finances and balance our checkbook. We can take joy in our bank statement and spending habits. We no longer have to fear money, because we have made it a part of our path.

## Our Body

The tiger is completely in tune with her body. If you have ever seen one up close, you have seen how comfortable she is in her skin. This is because she knows how important it is to attend to her physical well-being.

Imagine waking up in the morning after too little sleep, and realizing that you are already running late. There's no time for your previously scheduled morning meditation session. You roll out of bed, hastily get dressed, rush to your job, work so hard you forget about your lunch break, come home at the end of the day, and collapse on your sofa exhausted. You wanted to go to the gym after work, but at this point you are running on zero energy. You zone out for the rest of the night, end up going to bed late, and repeat the cycle the next day.

Sound familiar? The reason you have no mental or physical energy is because you did not attend to your body. No matter how flashy the energy drink commercials may be, no liquid is going to get you through a busy day unscathed and full of life. You can only do that by taking good care of yourself.

One way to cut through the busyness of your day is to include what are called the four exhilarations. Making sure we tend to these four aspects of our life gives us energy to handle whatever comes our way. They are:

1. Eating
2. Sleeping
3. Meditating
4. Exercising

While these four actions are something of a no-brainer, most of us end up skipping meals or shortchanging our sleep, believing all the while that we can get away with it. It's as if we think our bodies won't notice. We keep saying, "Tomorrow I'll do those things." After months of this, we realize that we are running out of tomorrows. We need to take care of our body today.

The trick is finding a way to slow down enough to squeeze in these four exhilarations, and most importantly, appreciate them. If you know you always have busy mornings, then you can apply discernment as to when you go to the grocery store. You can pick up breakfast food you don't need to cook, like a banana or cereal, so there is no excuse to not put something in your stomach first thing each morning. Even if you are just grabbing a breakfast bar and eating it on the train, try turning your attention to tasting your food and not just spacing out.

We all have a rough sense as to how much sleep we need, and yet we either shortchange ourselves until we run ragged, or sleep in and end up walking through our day in a haze. In either case, we end up a zombie. Once we figure out how much sleep we require, we can apply a sense of discipline and cut other activities short to insure we are taking care of our basic needs.

In an ideal world, we could roll out of bed in the morning and meditate for an hour before going to work. That does not often happen. But even squeezing in ten minutes before rushing into your daily routine, or ten minutes right when you get home at night, cuts through the speed of your daily life and energizes you so you can move forward with whatever comes next.

Exercising is a way to exert our body in a way other than our normal activity. Most of us sit still all day. To get up and go for a jog is offering a gift to yourself. You free yourself from lethargy and rouse a sense of energy in the midst of your day. Going for a run can also free you from the habit of always being in your head.

If you find you don't have time to run or hit the gym, do something simple. If you know yoga, you can get up from your desk and do a few simple postures. If yoga isn't your thing, just stretch or do some jumping jacks. Taking even five minutes out of your day to exercise your body provides far more energy than a Red Bull ever could.

Even though these four exhilarations are tremendously simple, including all of them in your day gives you the power to move through life with confidence and care.

## Our Travel

> May those who lose their way and wander
> In the wild find fellow travelers.
> And safe from threat of thieves and savage beasts,
> May they be tireless and their journey light.
>
> —*Shantideva*

For many of us, travel is an experience of anxiety. One of my teachers, Khenpo Tsultrim Gyamtso Rinpoche, once remarked that when he was growing up, people may have disliked travel, but they did not need to fear going up into the sky and dying in large groups. That very sentence may bring up anxiety for some of us. Between the fear of flying and the tight security we encounter at airports and train stations, traveling has become something of an ordeal. The important thing is to apply the gentleness of the tiger to these situations. You can be gentle with yourself and apply the techniques listed in chapter 5 to whatever anxiety may arise. You should also try to remain present with everyone you encounter. It could be the passenger sitting next to you on your flight, or the baggage claim attendant whose primary job is to deal with very annoyed people with lost luggage. To muster a seed of your own sanity and offer it to these individuals is a wonderful kindness.

There are many more ways we can apply the qualities of the tiger to our path of warriorship. You can ask yourself, "What kind of suit would the warrior who embodies a tiger wear?" or "What kind of music embodies the tiger's precision?" For my part, I would say earth tones and classical, but it's not up to me. While suggestions can be made about the practical applications of these teachings, it is up to you and you alone to determine how to apply them to your life.

You may make mistakes along the way. Doing so only means that you have joined the great lineage of meditators that has existed over the last several thousand years. Each meditation master in the past has led their life by learning from their mistakes, and applying the qualities of the tiger to further wake up to their heart and mind. Their stories of inner change are inspiring, because about half the time these stories are about how they messed up.

We have a long path ahead of us, and as we travel this path, our mistakes should be embraced and our discipline applied further. We can learn from the masters of the past and not become dissuaded from the path just because we are still schmucks a few months down the road. While we may still be schmucks, we are much kinder and more mindful schmucks than we used to be, and that's a start.

Our path not only includes but is based on the fact that we need to apply the qualities of the tiger to our home, our clothes, our financial situation, and all the nitty-gritty details of our life. As Sakyong Mipham Rinpoche has said, "The environment is a support or a deterrent for whatever we want to do. Everything in our environment—food, clothing, places, the hours we keep, the compassion or jealousy of others—affects us." Attending to the details of our environment is a crucial step along the warrior's journey. When we get our act together, we can be of great benefit to the world around us.

PART TWO

# HOW TO SAVE THE WORLD

# 8 / A SOCIETY BASED ON AN OPEN HEART

You can help the world. You, you, you, you, and you—all of you—can help the world. You know what the problems are. You know the difficulties. Let us do something. Let us not chicken out. Let us actually do it properly. Please, please, please!

—*Chögyam Trungpa Rinpoche*

In 2003, Sakyong Mipham Rinpoche called forth the young people of the Shambhala Buddhist tradition for a weekend retreat. Two hundred people showed up, eagerly anticipating what advice he might have to impart to us. Some of us were hoping he would tell us what we should do for a living. Others were figuring out what sort of relationship they wanted to have with their lovers. Others just wanted general guidance on how to live a good Buddhist lifestyle.

After waiting what seemed an eternity, the Sakyong took his seat, looked out at the crowd, and instead of giving us an instruction manual for our life, he said, "I am going to create an enlightened society. And you are going to help me do that, right?"

The crowd, not surprisingly, sat mute, blown away by the implications of his statement. He leaned in farther and very pointedly said, "Right?"

To which we all replied, "Of course!"

## CREATING AN ENLIGHTENED SOCIETY

The notion of an enlightened society is not some magical community wherein everyone has attained nirvana, or even has the perfect job or relationship. An enlightened society is actually very practical: it is a society based on having an open heart. During the Buddha's lifetime, King Dawa Sangpo approached the Awakened One and said, "I need help governing my kingdom. I want to pursue a spiritual life, but I can't take on robes and leave my subjects behind."

The Buddha sent his monastic attendants out of the room, and bestowed what are now known as the Kalachakra teachings on Dawa Sangpo. After receiving these in-depth instructions from the Buddha, King Dawa Sangpo knew how to rule in a benevolent and kind manner. He returned home and governed his kingdom in a way that inspired his subjects. They were encouraged to shift their attention away from their own concerns, and instead to think about the good of the society as a whole. The kingdom, which came to be known as Shambhala, was a land where everyone lived in a sane and compassionate manner.

To have a high spiritual teacher such as Sakyong Mipham Rinpoche turn to you and say, "I'm going to work to build that kind of enlightened society. Are you in?" can be mind-blowing. Many of us come to meditation just because we are stressed-out or want to take better care of ourselves. Yet at a certain point in your spiritual journey, you can no longer ignore all the suffering that surrounds you. Compassion blossoms naturally as you start to recognize the suffering in the world, and then one day you realize that your path is not just about your own situation, it's about creating a difference in our world. You are inspired to follow in the footsteps of the citizens of Shambhala by turning your attention toward helping others.

I don't think it is just meditators who are interested in changing the world for the better. We all want that. Even political nut jobs want to make the world a better place; they just want the world to resemble their personal vision of it. When you slow down and ponder how to make the world a bit better, you may come to the same conclusion that so many Buddhist masters in the past have come to: we cannot base the change we want to see in speed and aggression, but rather on compassionate wisdom.

It's hard to find a way to do that, particularly given the fact that our role models are few and far between. The remarkable thing is that as our society currently stands, famous people are often famous for all the wrong reasons. It is not that they are talented in a given field, but rather that they are rich or they film themselves having sex. Between the tabloids and gossip websites, these people get promoted to an almost godlike celebrity status. The celebrity heirs and heiresses of the world are looked up to by the masses, who envy the celebrities' lifestyle while simultaneously taking pleasure in their countless humiliations.

Meanwhile, the local hero serving in the military overseas is left to his own devices once he returns home. The family that volunteers each weekend at the homeless shelter in their neighborhood rarely receives the recognition they deserve. The single mother can't get someone to watch her kid for free so that she can go to the movies once a month. People who work diligently on humanistic fronts rarely receive so much as a thank-you, and there are no websites tracking their everyday activity and no eye-catching headlines: OLIVER BUYS HOMELESS MAN A SANDWICH: HOMELESS MAN SAYS THANK YOU.

I have to believe that anyone interested in pursuing spirituality, even if they are somewhat attracted to the celebrity culture of our times, ultimately wants to live in a world where the priorities are different than what they see in that culture. If current polling data is correct, most Americans do want to volunteer more, to offer themselves and their hearts to the community in which they live. Our society seems to just keep getting in the way of that aspiration.

Throughout the world, countries use a very particular marker for their success: the Gross Domestic Product

(GDP). In other words, the more your nation produces, the more successful it is. As citizens of these countries, we naturally use similar markers to judge our own status. If we have a good job, a nice house or apartment, a luxury car, and a beautiful spouse, we think we are successful. Yet many of us say we are unhappy.

In 1972, the king of Bhutan, Jigme Singye Wangchuck, instituted a different marker for success for his country: the Gross National Happiness (GNH) index. The four pillars of GNH are cultivating sustainable development, preserving cultural values, taking good care of the environment, and establishing a benevolent government.

While some of these markers are an attempt at gauging the happiness of the populace, many of them point to the idea that in order to be truly happy, you have to take care of other members of your society and the environment in which you live. In the United States, we are surrounded by people who have bought into the idea that "success" and "happiness" can be obtained by having a luxury vehicle and a penthouse apartment. We constantly try to meet those markers of joy by searching for one more thing that we can tack on to who we think we are. We are always focusing on external factors with the belief that they will lead to true and everlasting happiness for "me."

Worrying solely about "me" gets tiresome after a while. In order to really create positive change in the world, we need to shift our focus away from only thinking about ourselves. Sakyong Mipham Rinpoche wrote:

> We think, "Will this food make me happy? Will this movie make me happy? Will this person make me happy? Will this new sweater make me happy?" "What about me?" becomes the motivating force of our activity.[1]

In order to create a society that is based on bravery and kindness, we need to transition away from always thinking just about "me." Currently many of us wake up in the morning and say, "I hope I have a good day." We get to work and say, "I hope I get the praise I deserve. I hope this work I am doing will make me richer." We get home and say, "I'm exhausted and I need to take care of myself. I need to have a beer and watch TV and zone out to feel better about this day I've had." Day after day of looking out only for ourselves can be exhausting. Creating this cocoon of always thinking about "me" can be exhausting.

Imagine what it would be like if one day everyone woke up and decided to shift the focus of their day away from always holding themselves at the center of the universe. What if each of us made our day about benefiting others? Turning your attention from only taking care of yourself to taking care of others is the subtle distinction between the Hinayana (narrow vehicle) teachings and the Mahayana (greater vehicle) teachings. The distinction lies between the Hinayana view of being concerned only with our own path to awakening, and the Mahayana view of taking others' happiness as that path.

The more we become familiar with our own emotional ups and downs, the more we begin to see them in others. Previously we felt a deep anger for our coworker Brett. He took credit for our efforts, spread office gossip, and generally did not do any real work. Because we have trained ourselves on the cushion to recognize our strong emotions, acknowledge them, and come back to the present moment, we begin to see ourselves take the same gentle approach to our emotions at work. We take some space from our anger when we are confronted by Brett's meddling. When we are not so caught up in our own inner turmoil, we begin to see Brett's turmoil as well. Since we are no longer shooting daggers at Brett with our eyes, our gaze rests on his desk and we notice that the picture of his wife has disappeared. Because we are not focused on thinking up rebuttals to whatever he says, we begin to hear a slight sadness and desperation in his voice.

Soon enough, we find that Brett has been going through his own emotional upheavals: he feels trapped in his job, his wife just asked for a divorce, and he suffers from panic attacks. We have gone through similar experiences in the past, and all of a sudden we feel our heart opening to Brett. Our coworker may be acting in a spiteful or jealous manner, but it is only because he is suffering, *just like us.* When we see Brett not as a threat but as a fellow suffering human being, our heart breaks for him.

When we encounter difficult people, we often do not naturally experience this heart-opening quality. In that case, it may be helpful to engage in a contemplation practice.

## CONTEMPLATION PRACTICE FOR RELATING WITH DIFFICULT PEOPLE

First, take a good meditation posture and practice shamatha meditation for at least five minutes.

Now, think of a time when you acted in a manner similar to the way the difficult person in your life is acting. It may be a time when you felt underprepared, heartbroken, or so frustrated you couldn't even sleep. Rouse a memory that is juicy, and sit with whatever visceral feeling arises.

Once you have something potent to work with, begin this fortune cookie contemplation. A fun game some people engage in when they break open a fortune cookie is to add "in bed" to the end of their fortune. For example, "You will soon have great success . . . in bed." In this fortune cookie contemplation, though, you take on the feelings that arise around the difficult people in your life, and add the phrase "just like me." For example: "Brett sometimes will lash out for no reason . . . just like me." Or "He will try to promote his ideas so he can get ahead . . . just like me."

Stay with the scenario you originally began contemplating. After a little while exploring some of the seemingly negative things you and Brett have in common, you might find yourself moving on to more general assumptions about Brett: "He is trying to be happy . . . just like me."

Notice whatever inclination comes up in terms of discovering what you and Brett might share. Over time, you may find that you have more in common with this difficult person than you previously thought. While you may have different points of view or take different tactics at work, his motivations for doing what he does are not that different from your own.

Developing compassion for another person in this way is not a patronizing activity. It is not "I am so enlightened, and you suffer so much, so I will have pity for you." It's the realization that we're not better than anyone else. Actually we're all the same, because we all want the same thing: joy.

## Developing Bodhichitta

As discussed in the section exploring the tiger, true joy does not come from acquiring new gadgets or starting another steamy romance, but from being present with your life. It comes from turning your attention away from always thinking about yourself, and opening to the world around you.

The heart that yearns to connect with your world and to help others is known in the Buddhist tradition as *bodhichitta*. *Bodhichitta* is a Sanskrit word that can be translated as "awake heart." Through slowing down and being present with your world, you are more open to the suffering around you. Your heartstrings can be pulled by the simplest things: a puppy waiting to be adopted or a beautiful flower just beginning to blossom. While you may previously have walked right by these things, now you are open and available to your world. You feel an inherent richness and tenderness. This is bodhichitta.

Bodhichitta is inherent to who we are. It can be thought of as our unique "soft spot." We have all touched it before at some point in our life. Bodhichitta is our capacity to love and be loved.

However, just because we have been practicing and might occasionally feel our heart opening does not mean we can constantly rest in that feeling. All too often, the awakened heart can become shrouded by fear, or by a cocoon of opinions. Whenever we put ourselves before our fellow human beings, or tune out from our world because we don't want to deal with it, we are forming protective layers around our heart. We are creating a cocoon of fear and "me"-ness. Thus, bodhichitta is not just an openhearted state, but something we continuously cultivate through our meditation practice.

## CONTEMPLATION PRACTICE ON OPENING THE HEART

Take a few minutes now to sit where you are. You don't necessarily have to practice shamatha meditation, but just be present. It doesn't matter if you are on a crowded train, at work, or just sitting on your couch. Just be present with your body and your environment.

After settling your mind a bit, contemplate the question, "What is my experience of an awakened heart?" Let the question roll around your mind a bit. See what comes up. Are there images or memories that come to mind that inspire this feeling in you?

After sitting with this experience for a few minutes, just relax. Drop the question itself and just return to your breath. Particularly focus on the out-breath and the sensation of your breath moving out from your body into space.

## REMAINING OPEN IN THE FACE OF AGGRESSION

Bodhichitta may be the most important thing in the entire Buddhist canon. Without opening our heart to others, we become rigid meditators, only looking out for "me." At the weekend retreat where the Sakyong invited us to join him in creating an enlightened society, he went on to teach about bodhichitta. He taught that an open heart is the primary tool for creating a better world and an enlightened society.

Some people try to create positive change in society through engaging in protests or signing petitions. Other people try to support charities they believe are doing good work, or find a job in a field they think is beneficial to others. However, the simplest and most direct way to create positive change in the world is through connecting with our own awakened heart.

Our current society has told us that in order to be successful, we need to buy into the Gross Domestic Product mindset. We have been taught to believe we need to have lots of money and nice objects in order to be happy. Yet we have found that these things alone do not bring us joy. Simple acts of being present and compassionate bring us happiness. We find joy in being openhearted.

All too often we try to cover over this vulnerable heart in an attempt to not get hurt. It's only natural to want to shrink away from being open and genuine all the time when the world is filled with aggression. However, developing a willingness to be vulnerable is no different from developing a willingness to be alive. If we continually try to protect ourselves, if we always attempt to avoid embarrassment, challenge, or chaos, we will find ourselves trapped in a prison of our own defenses. Although nothing can get through to threaten us, we cannot feel anything, either. It is the path of the warriors to poke through their cocoon of defenses and share their heart with the world.

I once heard a story about a Catholic priest who wanted to have his last words recorded. This is what he said: As a young man, he had an aspiration to change the world. Yet the more he struggled, the more confused he became as to why he could not create positive change. Then as a middle-aged man, he thought that the road to changing the world was to encourage good behavior in his friends and family. After toiling away on that front for years, he again became discouraged.

Only when he was an old man at the end of his life did he realize that in order to create change in the world, he first needed to create change within. Having connected with his own vulnerable heart, he infused his friends and family with positive influence, and from there touched many people.

Similarly, in 2003, Sakyong Mipham Rinpoche looked out at the audience of two hundred young meditators and said, "A lot of times people think that they have to be enlightened to make a big difference in the world. They say, 'Well, I can help out when I've meditated a lot more, and studied more, and done many more retreats.' We can get very old doing all that. We have to make a change now. It has to be now."

You may not have spent years meditating or received instruction from all the best teachers in all the various philosophical schools. That does not mean you can't open your heart to the world and make a difference. You don't have to wait until you're enlightened. You don't have to ask anyone's permission. You just have to offer yourself, as you are, and allow your vulnerable heart to transform the world.

# 9 / MANIFESTING THE QUALITIES OF THE SNOW LION

As we begin to engage the Mahayana path, we can look to the second of the four dignities: the snow lion. Take a moment to visualize the spacious peaks of highland mountains where the atmosphere is clear, the air easy to breathe. This vibrant grassy area is punctuated with wildflowers, occasional trees, boulders and rocks. This is the peaceful home of the snow lion.

You may have seen snow lions on the flag of Tibet or even in statues outside your local library. Playful and energetic, the snow lion is white, muscular, and has a turquoise mane. She is said to leap from mountaintop to mountaintop. In traditional references, it is said that as the snow lion leaps, her mane is fanned by herbal winds.

Whenever I hear the phrase "fanned by herbal winds," I can't help but think of the Herbal Essences shampoo commercials, which begin with a woman looking very sad because her hair is flat and boring. She is introduced to Herbal Essences, and seconds later she is bouncing around, perky as can be, because her hair has been restored to its full potential.

When we discuss the snow lion, this image can be useful. At this point we know that a shampoo will not bring us everlasting happiness. Even if Herbal Essences is a sensational shampoo, it can only bring some temporary sense of satisfaction; even that form of joy is impermanent. In order to find true joy, we need to look to the example of the snow lion. The snow lion shares the same perkiness that is displayed in the commercial. However, this perkiness stems not from acquiring a new shampoo, boyfriend, or house, but because she is not weighed down by negative emotions.

As we discussed in the tiger section, when we get hooked by strong emotions it can be exhausting. For example, say your parents or a friend e-mails you on a Friday night and says that you don't visit enough. First you might feel guilty, then frustrated, then you attempt to alleviate those feelings by going out and drinking too much, and the next thing you know you're puking your feelings into a toilet bowl. You e-mail them a tirade about how they have ruined your night, pass out on the computer, and wake up to both physical and emotional messes that are of your own creation.

If you want to look to the example of the snow lion, then your path is to not get hooked by that strong emotion in the first place. The snow lion is not plagued by being dragged around by her emotions, and as a result she remains vibrant, energetic, and youthful.

## Doubting Our Inherent Goodness

In Shambhala Buddhism, we say that a root emotion that weighs us down is doubt. When we receive a painful phone call or e-mail, it can strike us to the core; we thought we were a pretty decent person, but now we feel a fundamental disconnection from our own goodness. We may think, "If I was really in touch with my innate wisdom, I wouldn't be a prick to those I love." We lose faith in our ability to be kind, in our meditation practice, and especially in our own basic goodness. We are struck with a feeling of failure; that we have set out on a path to create joy for ourselves and be a good person, but ultimately it's just not possible. It's just too hard in this speedy, chaotic world to practice these principles of mindfulness and compassion. We may as well give up.

This doubt can suffocate us. However, acknowledging that we have fallen into this trap of doubt is the first step in working our way out of it. This level of exploring doubt is not about turning off our critical intelligence; quite the opposite. We need to begin our exploration of this disjunction between our innate goodness and our prickishness by wholeheartedly contemplating, "What is my experience of doubt? How does it affect me?" You don't even have to meditate or engage in a formal contemplation, but try taking a day or two to think through that very basic question.

There are a number of ways that doubt in our inherent goodness can manifest. Some of these may be familiar from your own experience of doubt:

*Anxiety.* With this manifestation of doubt, you feel some sense of not being comfortable with the way things are in your life. You wish it was easier to find someone you would like to date, that the people you meet wouldn't be so needy, that they would pick up the check once in a while, and so on. There is a general sense of unease where you want to change your situation, your friends, or yourself. No matter the scenario, you cannot trust in the situation as it is. In other words, you cannot trust the present moment.

*Jealousy.* This form of doubt involves your relationship with other people. Perhaps you have not felt included, loved, or appreciated at times. Coworkers go out to lunch without you, and you begin to wonder why you were not invited. You question your own self-worth. Out of that emotion comes the assumption that the world isn't treating you the way you expected it to. You are disappointed, and you are envious of people who you perceive are better off.

*Forgetfulness.* Having fallen into the trap of doubt, you begin to slack off on mindfulness. You think that your meditation practice is something you can pick up right where you left off a month ago, as opposed to treating it as something you need to continuously practice. You begin to grow speedy, and you forget simple things like picking up milk, and as a result you end up drinking your coffee black for three days. You become absentminded and have no discipline in acknowledging the wonder of your life.

*Arrogance.* At some point, you may have started to think that your doubt is some great new philosophical discovery. In this particular trap, you believe that your confusion and lack of faith in basic goodness could be a brand-new religion. You think, "Yeah, yeah, yeah, the Buddha and some of the greatest minds of the last twenty-six hundred years have encouraged me to discover my buddha nature, but I've discovered something they never experienced: 'basic apathy.'" You begin to propagate your view on basic goodness to whoever will listen to you with great (yet disingenuous) confidence.

*Slandering.* In this form of getting caught up in doubt, you look at your own goodness, your practice, your meditation teachers, and think that they have all failed you and are worthy of slander. You might see this sometimes with senior practitioners in a Buddhist community. They have been around the *sangha,* or community, for thirty years, but at some point they experienced this disconnection from the view of basic goodness. As a result they do not believe it is their own fault that they no longer practice, but instead they blame the Buddhist sangha or organization they are a part of. They begin to criticize the organizational structure, the way the dharma is taught, or the organization's teachers. Because they are trapped by their own doubt, they solidify it and begin to criticize and gossip about anyone who still believes in the teachings.

*No synchronization of mind and body.* In this manifestation of doubt, you are so upset by your emotional states that you can't even keep yourself together. You are so caught up in your head that you can walk from your home to work or school, and you don't even notice that the cherry trees are in full bloom. You are so caught up in yourself that you can't even pour a cup of tea properly; the hot water just splashes into the saucer while you ramble on to a friend about your most recent drama.

## DOUBT AND ROMANTIC RELATIONSHIPS

One category of experience that causes many of us to fall into the trap of doubt is romantic relationships. Once you get weighed down by that initial strong hook of doubt in connection with such a relationship, you can experience all of the above manifestations of doubt.

Let me paint you a picture: Your boyfriend steps out for the night with some friends. You try to reach him, but keep getting his voice mail. Sure, logic dictates that he is probably at some underground bar or his phone is on mute, but something in you starts to stir. You begin to get a bit anxious: "Where is he? What is he doing? Why is he ignoring me?" Maybe you're more the jealous type: "Is he dancing with other women? Buying them drinks? What if he gets really drunk and one of them tries to kiss him?" From there you get indignant: arrogance flares up and you think, "Who is he to ignore me? What, he thinks he can cheat on me? *Me?*"

Before you know it, you've forgotten everything you wanted to do that night and are writing him a slanderous text message, complaining about how poorly he treats you and what a jerk he is. You're so angry and caught up in this situation that you can't do anything but lie in bed. You're paralyzed by your emotions, and have lost all awareness of how to treat your mind or body.

Does this sort of emotional flare-up sound familiar to you? I believe we have all experienced at least some of these emotional explosions. Many Tibetan Buddhist teachers have noted that as a culture, we Westerners don't have a lot of faith in our innate wisdom and goodness. We tend to loathe ourselves to a certain extent, and not trust in simple things like the fact that we deserve to be loved and respected.

This is where the path of the snow lion comes in. The path of the snow lion is catching yourself before you fall into the trap of doubt. The snow lion has great confidence in herself. You can remind yourself to come back to the knowledge that you are worth being loved. You are genuinely a good person. You possess buddha nature.

Furthermore, when obstacles arise, instead of getting weighed down by them, you can consider the idea that maybe the story line you've created is not necessarily related to reality. Many internal story lines are not rooted in our basic sanity or wisdom, but rather in our confusion. When your boyfriend calls you three hours later from an unknown phone number saying just how much he misses you and how sad he was when his cell phone battery died, it might be a good time to consider a path that allows you the freedom to escape the trap of doubt.

## The Tools of the Snow Lion

There are a few tools the snow lion engages in order to remain free from the trap of doubt, and stay perky enough to leap from mountaintop to mountaintop. I will give you a brief introduction to these tools now, and then we'll explore them more fully in the next three chapters.

### Compassion

When we open our heart fully to others, we naturally move beyond any tendency to only think about "me." We can practice simple acts like smiling, listening deeply to those people whose company we enjoy (and those we don't), or a simple meditation practice I like to call Not Saying No.

The general idea is that throughout our day we are bombarded with opportunities to stop thinking only about ourselves. However, we are often dismissive of them. Try taking one day to practice not immediately saying "no" to the many requests that get thrown at you. It can be simple things like when someone drops a pencil near you, and you go out of your way to retrieve it. It can be holding the elevator for someone even when you are in a rush. Alternatively, it can be offering each homeless person you encounter a little change or a dollar.

Obviously, if someone approaches you and says, "Let's go have anonymous, dangerous sex on a pile of needles," have some common sense and take care of yourself by refusing. In the Not Saying No exercise, we are talking about just pushing the envelope slightly in terms of being open and compassionate. It is based on taking care of yourself (the core Hinayana discipline) so that you are able to take care of others.

At the end of a day of practicing Not Saying No, set aside some time to notice how you feel. Going beyond your normal comfort level and being charitable with your heart can be liberating.

## DISCIPLINE OF VIRTUE

There are times when life hands us lemons. It is simplistic to expect you to take all the lemons of samsara and make lemonade out of them; after all, we are still progressing on the spiritual path. However, there are times when we are faced with negative situations where we can relate directly with them, even just by letting them exist. Sometimes we can be brave and go a little bit beyond what we normally do in order to apply virtue to the situation.

This is not a moralistic sense of "I am good, you are bad, so I will always point out when you mess up." That is ego based and arrogant. Instead, this application of virtue involves discipline; we need to be sharp in pinpointing how best to act in any given situation.

Utilizing the discernment of the tiger, we know how we want to act and what we want to refrain from. The path of the snow lion is acting on that discernment and actually following through. We can look at how our behavior affects others and, in an attempt to be compassionate, act in a way that we deem wholesome and beneficial.

## THE SIX PARAMITAS

There are six more tools that the snow lion carries on her metaphorical tool belt: generosity, discipline, patience, joyous exertion, meditation, and *prajna* (superior knowledge). These are generally referred to in Buddhist texts as the six *paramitas*, or perfections. We do not need to be perfect to engage any of them, but they are helpful in creating perfect conduct in an otherwise imperfect world.

In looking to be of benefit to others and be of service to the world, we can look to each of these qualities and examine which is appropriate to any given situation. Some may be clear, such as applying patience when your friend is taking too long getting ready and so you are afraid you will be late to your dentist appointment. Other situations may require more thought, such as how best to exert yourself in a tricky task at work without pissing other people off. However, these six paramitas are applicable to anything we face, and are the snow lion's go-to tools for all projects.

In order to experience joy, we have to preserve our dignity. It's difficult to hang out with someone who is lost in self-doubt. If someone is constantly running themselves down and getting upset over little things, they drain their own energy, as well as the energy of everyone around them. You don't have to be like that; you are not inherently like that. You are basically good. In our journey of emulating the snow lion, our practice is to come back to the essential point of our basic goodness and to develop faith in this.

Returning to the reality of our situation and the world around us is a reminder that everything we experience can be part of our path. We do not have to be stuck on the "me" plan; we can upgrade to the "we" plan. When we apply our discipline and step out of the trap of doubt, we have a world waiting for us, hungry for our open heart. We can offer compassion, the discipline of virtue, and our tool belt of paramitas to make this world a better place. If we don't, who will?

# 10 / SEX, LOVE, AND COMPASSION

Being on the spot, even if it hurts, is preferable to avoiding.

—*Pema Chödrön*

One of the best ways to see compassion in action is through the example of engaging it in our romantic and sexual relationships. We can use the lessons we learn in these relationships and apply them to all of our interactions. We have all been hurt before. You likely have touched your soft spot, your bodhichitta, when you opened your heart to someone else and were ultimately disappointed. When you do get hurt, it is habitual to try to cover over your open heart. In other words, you close yourself off to others. You shut yourself off from feeling vulnerable in an attempt not to get hurt again.

After some time we all do heal, and more often than not, we once again strive to reopen our heart. There's a level of joy that comes from connecting with other people in this way that we don't want to miss out on.

Wanting to be in love is natural to the human experience. We all want to love. We love love. However, its highs are dizzying, its lows traumatic enough that we want to rid them from our memory. It almost seems counterintuitive to try to reach contentment and equanimity in our life while also cultivating this roller coaster of emotions.

To think that we need to sort our romantic life into one category of our being and our spiritual growth into another would be a mistake. It is through applying basic Buddhist principles that we can use relationships with others as part of our path. With care and consideration of your partner, falling in love does not have to be such a roller coaster; we just have to learn to handle our expectations.

## Falling (and Staying) in Love— and Beyond

When you offer your love to a partner, at first it's very exploratory. You are curious about your partner. You want to know more about their past, their family, and their odd little habits. You try new food at their suggestion, go to unfamiliar places, and it is all very exciting. You begin to learn all sorts of things about your partner. Elizabeth's favorite type of ice cream is chocolate and her favorite show is *Gossip Girl*. She dresses in this way and likes those sorts of people and never drinks that sort of soft drink.

At some point, these aspects of your partner are likable but they are not necessarily new and exciting anymore; you do not apply the same level of curiosity as you once did to the relationship since you already know so much about your lover. Later on down the road, you may just stop being curious about your partner altogether.

I was watching a television program the other day where an old married couple was fighting. In an attempt to ameliorate the situation, the husband brought his wife a cosmopolitan, saying he knows how much she loves them. "Oh!" she exclaimed sarcastically, "You remembered! I haven't had one of these in twenty years!" An argument of course immediately followed, based in the all-too-simple truth that sometimes we just stop inquiring who it is we are spending our life with and, as a result, we stop noticing when things change.

Often we take our partner for granted when we should

be seeing them as a principle object of our compassion. The Tibetan word for compassion is *nyingje,* which can be more directly translated as "noble heart." This is a helpful term when thinking about bringing compassion into our most intimate relationships: we need to fully offer those closest to us our noble heart.

Curiosity is a form of compassion. I believe many long-term couples continue to be excited by their partner, but they don't follow up by inquiring just how their partner has changed. As meditators on the path, we know that all things are impermanent. We have an understanding that everything shifts and is in transition around us. We have no trouble seeing our own bodies and library of knowledge develop and change. Yet to think that our partners change just as fluidly as we do can be shocking. It is the truth, though, that although we think the same dependable person we dine with every night is one solid thing, they are in fact a conglomeration of experiences and knowledge that is constantly shifting, not unlike the seasons themselves. To solidify such a person is nonsense, yet we are all guilty of falling into that trap at one point or another.

Somewhere in the midst of a relationship, certain expectations are set up. You don't draft a contract or divvy up who does what, but at the same time you begin to believe that your partner owes you certain things. Those certain things extend beyond just loving you and being open and honest with you. A dangerous word starts to get used: "always."

"You *always* get home first—why didn't you call if you knew you were going to be late tonight?"

"You *always* leave the laundry for me to fold—why can't you fold it too?"

"You *always* say that when I want to try something new."

When the expectations in a relationship get too fixed, they create the same destructive power as stuck emotions. Like stuck emotions, fixed expectations drag us down, causing doubt and anxiety to fill our beings. We begin to close off our heart and fend for ourselves instead of being available to hear our partner out. We stray from the quality of unconditional openheartedness that makes us want to help the people we love, even at our own expense. We are turning away from our bodhichitta, shutting down our ability to act in a compassionate manner. When you see yourself starting to stray from compassionate activity, you know your relationship is in trouble.

At the point where you find yourself closing down from communicating openly in a relationship, you have a choice about how you would like to proceed. One way forward is to lay fresh layers of protection around your vulnerable heart. You are dampening the other person's ability to hurt you, but you are also less able to communicate your own love genuinely. You are essentially preparing yourself for an inevitable breakup.

The alternative is loosening up your expectations and reconnecting with that curiosity you were able to offer at the beginning of the relationship. You commit to exploring where you are stuck, where you have put up that protective shielding, and how you can open yourself more to your partner. This is a way to deepen a relationship, by recommitting to applying gentle curiosity toward learning about your lover.

The same openhearted curiosity can be applied when considering a compassionate way to enter the dating scene. I have heard so many single people say that they are holding out for Mr. or Ms. Right. If only they could go to the right bar, or the right singles night, or the right website, then that Mr. or Ms. Right would be there waiting for them. As the Buddhist master Dzongsar Khyentse Rinpoche once said about romance, "The problem is not that the right situations don't arise. It's not really that. But we always have a certain expectation, we have hopes and fears. And those lead to disappointments."

When we solidify what we hope to find in a romantic partner, we are heading for a rocky road. We can make a checklist of what we are looking for in terms of physical appearance, intelligence, sense of humor, religious preference, and so on. We think that if we can find all of those qualities in someone, then they are the perfect person for us.

If we strictly adhere to such a list, we are setting ourselves up for failure. Instead, you can remain willing to keep an open mind. You can explore everyone you encounter without a hidden agenda or a checklist. You may end up meeting someone who flies in the face of what you think you need in your life to be happy, but who is indeed the perfect person for you. Through keeping an open mind and heart, you may find true happiness where you least expect it.

## COMPASSIONATE SEXUAL ACTIVITY

One tricky area of opening our heart revolves around sex. Sex is experienced as different things by different people. It can be used to show true love or affection. It can be used simply to have fun. It can be used to smooth things over when you have gotten into a fight with your spouse or as an excuse to indulge your laziness and not get out of bed. It can be a wonderful, painful, humiliating, and at times, I would posit, a compassionate activity.

In terms of Buddhism and sex, we know for a fact that even the historical Buddha, Siddhartha Gautama, had intercourse. While growing up in his palace, he apparently had a large harem of women. Some texts state that these women were simply dancing girls, others that they were courtesans who would please the prince in more carnal ways. In either case, we know that our friend Siddhartha had sex because his wife, Yasodhara, eventually gave birth to a son, and as far as I know, sex is generally how children are created.

Flash forward to when Siddhartha became a buddha, and suddenly he had a number of people coming to him, trying to live a spiritual life. He realized that his monastic followers would have to abide by certain rules, principle among them the five precepts.

The five precepts are: not taking the life of sentient beings, not taking what is not offered, not engaging in sexual misconduct, not using mindless speech (slander, gossip, lying, idle speech), and not ingesting intoxicants. We will be focusing on the third precept: *kāmesu micchācāra veramanī sikkhāpadaṃ samādiyāmi,* or "I take the vow to abstain from engaging in sexual misconduct."

All five of these precepts have been interpreted in numerous ways over time and in different cultures. In the West there are some Buddhist communities where monastics vow to abide by these rules, but lay practitioners do not. Some communities encourage their lay practitioners to work with the precepts on an ongoing basis, while others utilize them only in long-term retreat situations.

I think any contemplation of these precepts can be helpful for a practitioner, so long as they take them to heart. However, I cannot imagine that the Buddha laid out these precepts so that thousands of years later his followers could fight over the "right" way to utilize them. If anything, I think the story of the Buddha's teaching career serves as a signal about how we can explore the meaning of sexual misconduct for ourselves.

As we mentioned earlier, following his enlightenment, the Buddha set out to find the handful of ascetics with whom he had practiced meditation before. They were quite down on Siddhartha Gautama because the last time they saw him, he had abandoned the path of strict asceticism, a sign that he clearly was going nowhere on the spiritual path.

As the Buddha approached his fellow meditation practitioners, they saw a marked change in his appearance. He had a great joy and presence to him, which was extremely magnetizing. They began to move closer to him, and begged him to teach them how he had achieved such mastery over his own mind. Instead of giving them precepts or set disciplines then and there, he extended an invitation by saying, "Come and see for yourself."

With that invitation in mind, I think it is important to determine what compassionate sexual behavior is on an individual level. In fact, we could switch a negative disciplinary idea into a positive force for our health. Instead of contemplating how we can "abstain from sexual misconduct," we should endeavor to come up with a way to promote positive sexual relations.

Attempting to develop a path for compassionate sexual activity is not easy. It's hard to sort through the many volumes of teachings on new ideas for making love. Furthermore, we are constantly bombarded by negative sexual imagery on television, the Internet, and magazines.

It is important to find our own style for bringing compassion into the bedroom. It can be openly communicating with your lover about what you are comfortable with. Alternatively, it can be creating a safe space within which the two of you can be fully present with each other. It is up to each of us to determine what exactly compassionate sex means to us.

## ONE-NIGHT STANDS: VIEW, ACTIVITY, AND FRUITION

One question that often comes my way is whether you can be a "good" Buddhist and still have one-night stands. Personally, I think it's possible if you seriously consider your view, activity, and the fruition of this sort of situation.

### VIEW

The important thing in any sexual activity, casual or in a long-term relationship, is considering your own motivation. Are you interested in having a one-night stand because you are too busy for a relationship, but you appreciate the other person and want to make a sexual connection with them? If so, that is one motivation worth acknowledging. Another motivation might be, "I'm drunk. I'm horny. They're hot." That motivation strikes me as likely to lead to trouble.

Knowing your motivation before engaging in any act is important, and this is doubly so when you are involving another person in potentially risky behavior such as sex. There are emotional risks as well as physical ones, so knowing your own intention is key.

### ACTIVITY

Conduct is important. In my mind there are two ways to get enlightened. The first is to sit your butt down and practice meditation nonstop until you reach full awakening. The other is to bring meditation into your conduct, applying the principles you develop on the cushion to every aspect of your life.

When it comes to sex, good conduct could mean being very open and straightforward with your partner. It could be telling them very clearly about your intentions, or making sure you practice safe sex. Being openhearted, genuine, and caring seems simple enough, but it is especially important if you are attempting to bring someone to your bedroom.

### FRUITION

This may be the simplest marker of whether you have pulled off a compassionate one-night stand. Quite simply, you can examine how you feel the morning after. Applying curiosity to your own state, you can see if you find elation or humiliation. If it's the latter, you likely won't want to attempt such a thing again. It's unfortunate if you feel this way, but mistakes along the path are helpful; now you know something you never want to do again, and you can vow not to repeat the same set of actions. If you feel elation, however, you may be one of those rare people who can casually have sex.

When it comes to sex, it seems that the looser you get in terms of the relationship structure, the more likely you are to cause harm either to yourself or your partner. Much of this harm can be prevented by openly communicating with your lover. It is essential to any relationship, no matter how long it runs the course, to remain open and curious about each other and how you are both changing with time. Keeping this curiosity allows you to refrain from developing set expectations that box your partner into a corner where they have no hope of satisfying your needs.

In sex and in love we have one tool that can uplift our situation and bring us indestructible joy: bodhichitta. Because it is inherent to all beings, we can explore how to open our heart and how we can connect with the hearts of people we love and make love to. Opening the heart, without conditions, is our path. It is the compassionate way to live in our world. We may get hurt, but if we want to grow and find true love, or strive to love all beings, bodhichitta is the way to go.

# 11 / HOW TO APPLY DISCIPLINE, EVEN WHEN YOUR HEAD GETS CUT OFF

I grew up attending a military high school. It was like a normal high school, except our mascot was the Cadet and we would drill with decommissioned rifles in Civil War uniforms once a week and in seasonal parades.

When I tell people about this, they are somewhat shocked, and they become completely bewildered when they learn that I enjoyed it. There was something about marching in unison with a number of people that engaged me. There was a certain discipline about the whole affair; you had to bring your mind and body in complete synchronicity. If you got lost in fantasy or drifted from the present moment in any way, you would find yourself out of step with the rest of your squad and it would look bad. In order to be good at drill, you need to be fully present. When everyone in the squad was able to be fully present and attentive to one another, the fluidity was mind-stoppingly gorgeous. Even though as individuals we were a bunch of awkward teenagers, when you put us together and applied a mind-body discipline, we radiated dignity.

*Discipline* is a word that has a bad reputation in the West. It often gets used as something that is inflicted on us by other people. A parent might discipline their child when the child is misbehaving, or a personal trainer might say we need more discipline at the gym if we want to lose weight. It feels as if discipline is something imposed on us. We know this form of discipline is for our own good, but that does not bring us joy.

## DISCIPLINE AS A SOURCE OF HAPPINESS

From a Buddhist point of view, discipline doesn't have to be a negative thing; it can be a direct source of happiness. When we apply discipline to our meditation practice, we are often left with a positive feeling. For early-rising meditators, there is the discipline that gets us out of bed in the morning. There is also a discipline that pushes us out of our habitual routine and makes time to get our butt on the cushion. Then we apply discipline in maintaining our posture, and continuously coming back to our breath for however long we practice. At the end of our meditation, we feel delighted because this form of discipline is something we cultivated ourselves, and most importantly, because it is rooted in virtue.

The discipline that is intimately connected with virtue is the type the snow lion applies to her life. One way to tell if discipline is connected to virtue is to consider whether it bears a feeling of gentleness. If it feels like you are being hard on yourself, this is likely a form of discipline that is rooted in aggression. Such neurotic strictness is based in your confusion. Instead, the snow lion bases her discipline in trust in her basic goodness.

The interesting thing about living in our modern world is that there are constant opportunities to test whether we are applying discipline in a gentle way or if we are closing off our heart and being aggressive. When you are faced with lust, anger, or prejudice, you can use these situations as opportunities for training in the discipline of virtue.

Virtue is not necessarily taking a moralistic point of view. Developing a set of highbrow standards is antithetical to the path of dharma. Holding tight to a set of opinions solidifies a sense of "me." It is not compassionate activity to wield a set of standards as a weapon against others. If you do this, you end up thinking less of people because you have developed a set of morals that others do not adhere to. This subjective idea of virtue is a quick way to build up your ego and cut yourself off from connecting with the people around you.

Instead, virtue in the Buddhist sense is the meditative warrior's skill in touching their own heart. Once you have learned about discernment, you can apply that tool to figure out on a case-by-case basis what you want to open yourself up to, versus what you know you need to move away from. Having explored what to accept and what to reject in your daily life, the path of the snow lion is to apply the discipline to follow through on those intentions. For example, it is easy to decide that your boyfriend is toxic to be around, but it's hard to actually end the relationship. Even if it is a great kindness to yourself and to your partner, it takes discipline to follow through and enter into the painful discussion that a breakup entails.

## Practices for Applying Virtuous Discipline

Continuously applying virtuous discipline is by no means an easy task. At times we all find ourselves surrounded by people who continue to put their own desires first, not necessarily caring who gets hurt so long as they get what they want.

The fourteenth-century meditation master Ngulchu Thogme knew this fact well, and he offered thirty-seven practices for a bodhisattva, or openhearted warrior, to engage in so they can live in an openhearted manner. Many of these practices revolve around applying virtue to even the toughest of situations. For example:

If someone cuts off your head
Even when you have not done the slightest thing wrong,
Through the power of compassion

To take his misdeeds upon yourself
Is the practice of a bodhisattva.[1]

In today's world, you are more likely to come across someone trying to nudge ahead of you in line at the movies than someone who wants to cut off your head. In either scenario, Ngulchu Thogme's point still stands. Here he is saying that no matter what someone does to you, including an act of violence, you still have an opportunity to respond with compassion.

Even if you are completely undeserving of the aggression brought on your head, you can attempt to be openhearted with this individual. You can understand that this person who has wronged you is confused. You can ask yourself if you think this person thoroughly analyzed what they were doing before acting, or if they were acting from their own stuck emotional state.

If and when you have realized that the other person is simply confused, you can empathize. You too have acted impulsively in the past, often without realizing the harm you caused people around you. Compassion naturally dawns from this empathy.

Let's take another example from Ngulchu Thogme's playbook:

Should someone slander you
Throughout a billion worlds,
With a heart full of love, to proclaim his good qualities
   in return
Is the practice of a bodhisattva.[2]

We have all been the subject of rumors that made us look mean or foolish. Ngulchu Thogme is saying that even if someone goes about trying to destroy your reputation, you don't necessarily need to respond by running around correcting people's perceptions of you. You also don't have to go punch the rumormonger in the nose. While it might be helpful to set the story straight when you can, running around and telling everyone that your adversary is despicable for spreading lies is not exactly the action of a bodhisattva.

Instead, we can recognize that this person is trying to gain attention in all the wrong ways, and we can try to come up with something about them that we think is worthy of praise. Here the discipline of virtue might mean opening our heart further in the midst of being attacked. When people approach you in an attempt to further the rift between you two, imagine how surprised they will be when you start singing your adversary's praises! You can attempt to clear your name in a variety of ways, but in order to truly shift the situation around, try being honest yet compassionate to the gossiper.

> If in the middle of a crowd of people
> Someone reveals your hidden faults and abuses you for
>     them,
> To see him as a spiritual friend and to bow with respect
> Is the practice of a bodhisattva.[3]

Here Ngulchu Thogme refers to an experience many of us have shared: You are out with people and someone calls you on your habitual shtick. Your impulse may be to change the subject or deny the accusation, but doing so only adds a fresh layer to the protective shielding you have built around your heart.

If someone points out a hidden fault of yours, even if they make fun of you for it, it's best to objectively ponder the point being made. You may find that the criticism is accurate. If this is the case, then we should not view our supposed tormentor as such, but truly see them as a spiritual friend. They have allowed you to learn something new about yourself.

Usually we would look to a mentor or spiritual teacher to point out our shortcomings and faults, and not a buddy from work or even a good friend. The discipline of applying virtue in this case is moving beyond our wounded pride, and acknowledging that anyone can serve as a teacher by offering us an opportunity for spiritual growth. Such an experience does not call for retaliation in any way, but instead gives you an opportunity to offer respect to your new spiritual friend.

## BENEFITS OF APPLYING VIRTUE

When we thoroughly apply the discipline of virtue, it is said that we experience the opposite of what it feels like to be trapped by doubt. Our faith in our own basic goodness grows. We utilize all our encounters as part of our path of virtue, and as a result we are like the snow lion, unencumbered by habitual mind, and free to traverse higher realms of emotional states. These virtues of the higher realms include:

*Basic upliftedness.* You experience a sense of being joyful. As a result of not being weighed down by only thinking about how to protect yourself, you have a great amount of energy for other activities.

*A sense of health and togetherness.* Part of having so much energy is that you can take good care of yourself. You respect yourself enough that you are inclined to eat well and exercise. You begin to see the big picture in all situations and are able to get your act together, representing yourself with great dignity.

*Precision and brilliance.* This is not brilliance as in being smart, but rather that you have a radiant quality. You become more precise in both your intentions and your deeds. That level of precision has a magnetizing, vivid quality to it.

*Availability to other people.* Because you are not constantly worried about looking out for just yourself, you have room in your heart to be available to everyone else around you. You move from looking out for yourself as number one, and instead treat everyone you encounter with that level of regard.

*Genuine goodness in behavior and demeanor.* You may not be concerned with a purely moral point of view, but if your actions are connected to basic goodness, then they naturally are good. People may begin to notice that your very demeanor is emanating goodness.

*Synchronization of body and mind.* You are able to accomplish so much because your mind and body are completely in sync. Just like the group of awkward teenage cadets turned dignified drill squad, there's a certain magic about your being. Even just walking down the street you have a certain bounce to your step, the bounce of the snow lion.

## RIDING THE WINDHORSE

The more we apply ourselves to virtue, the more we can ride the natural energy of our being, our *windhorse.* In Tibetan this is known as *lungta. Lung* can be translated as "energy," or "wind," and *ta* means "horse." Just like a horse, we can ride the energy of our life, staying with the magic that surrounds us in every moment.

The principle of windhorse is that we have an unceasing energy within us that we tap into throughout our day. Sometimes when we have closed ourselves off to the world around us, we say we feel "low energy." Really we are expressing that we are not in touch with our windhorse, our generator of energetic activity.

Through applying virtue, we experience windhorse. We feel connected to our world. Even when negative situations arise, we do not frown at them but see each one as an opportunity to open up our heart further. We apply the discipline of not escaping from the present moment, not running away from difficulty. Instead we lean in, opening further to the world, and riding the natural energy of our life.

# 12 / RIDING THE WAVES OF YOUR LIFE

Imagine sitting on a hot, crowded beach. As you look around, you see people bickering, lusting indiscriminately after one another, trying to find the best six-by-four strip of sand to claim as their own, rebuffing others' advances to come near them. The shore itself is littered with trash, and even sitting on it makes you uncomfortable. After dwelling on this dirty, gross beach for a while, you make a conscious effort to leave it behind.

You enter the ocean and swim vigorously away from the beach. You keep going, despite whatever waves come at you and try to knock you back. When a large wave approaches, you dive into it, utilizing it as a refreshing experience as opposed to treating it like an obstacle. When you do get turned around and see the beach, you feel only revulsion, which further propels you along your path away from it.

You begin to glimpse another shore in the distance, which inspires you to swim faster and harder than you ever have before. Eventually you make it to this new beach. The sand is beautiful, the air cool and crisp, and you delight in having left the shore of suffering behind.

As you look back at where you came from, though, your heart breaks because everyone is still on that beach, looking even more anguished than when you left them. You think, "If only the people over there realized they are suffering and exerted themselves, they too could come to this cool, pleasant shore." You wish to aid them in that process, and begin to swim back in an attempt to show them this other shore. This is the journey of the enlightened bodhisattva.

For many of us, we have already looked around and realized that our day at the beach doesn't look like it did in the brochure. There is pain, heartbreak, and aggression all around us. Like many great Buddhist masters before us, we feel a yearning to move away from that suffering. This is similar to entering into the ocean.

There is a story about the Buddha where he throws his offering bowl into the river and it skips upstream. In the same way, we realize that if we are going to move away from this shore of pain and anguish, we need to exert ourselves and enter into activity that is counter to the way people normally do things. When a big obstacle comes our way we don't try to avoid it; instead, we use it as part of our path. We dive into that wave of an obstacle, and come out the other end refreshed. When we see that others are still lost in their habitual patterns we feel for them, and we utilize this knowledge as fuel for trying to do something other than our habitual reactions.

For many of us, this is where we are on the path. We are out at sea, either working with the waves that buffer us back toward our habitual realm, or leaping into them and finding new, compassionate ways of relating to adversity. Somewhere in the midst of this long swim, we get that glimpse of the other shore and are inspired to go there. That other shore is enlightenment.

## TRAVELING TO THE OTHER SHORE

As we enter the path of the bodhisattva, there are six principles that can be incredibly helpful in our long journey toward awakening. These are the six *paramitas*, or transcendental actions. *Param* can be translated as "other shore," while *ita* means "arrived." It is through practicing these six perfections that we can skillfully navigate our way through the obstacles in our life, and ultimately arrive at the other shore of enlightenment.

These six paramitas help you loosen your ego and open your mind to a larger view, the view of unshakable awakening. They are generosity, discipline, patience, joyous exertion, meditation, and prajna (superior knowledge).

## GENEROSITY

The snow lion is exuberant because she is not holding on to anything. Strong emotions and doubt do not weigh her down, so why should she seek to hold on to any material possessions? She is incredibly generous because she knows that acting in this way only gives her more opportunities to become a kinder, better person. The path of the snow lion is noticing where you feel stingy in your life, and using that knowledge to offer yourself fully in those situations.

Generosity from a Buddhist point of view is not about helping someone who is beneath us. We are not offering a homeless person money because we think we are better than they are. We make offerings because we realize that on a heart level we all possess the same basic goodness.

At times we may feel strapped for cash or extremely busy. For years I chaired a committee of professional fund-raisers charged with the mission of brainstorming how to further stimulate generosity within a Buddhist community. When the economic crisis hit in 2008, we opened our annual meeting on a grim note: people could not offer money like they had in the past. As a result, some organizations we worked with that relied heavily on donations were suffering.

We had the opportunity to shut down and be very closed-minded about how to raise funds in this environment, but instead we took the opposite approach. Although we were charged with raising money, we felt people could offer so much more. It was then and there we adopted a new motto: "Everyone has something to give."

Generosity is based in knowing what you are capable of giving, and going just a little beyond that. It is having a bad month but knowing that other beings have it worse, and so you take time to help others, maybe volunteering at a local animal shelter. It is seeing your low bank balance, but offering your friend a loan because they are struggling even more than you are. It is feeling that you are running late, but staying with someone who is clearly in pain and eager to vent. Knowing what you can give has to be based in taking care of yourself, but it's also about knowing just how far you can go beyond your comfort level in order to be of benefit to others.

When times are especially tough, you may not be able to offer the homeless person on your corner money. When that happens, offer a smile. Offer eye contact, and say, "Sorry, but I can't help you today." Even when you cannot offer financial support, you can make an offering in the form of genuine interaction.

The idea of everyone having something to give is grounded in knowing that we are basically good. We can draw on the gentle strength of our basic goodness, and we can offer that in any scenario we encounter. When we are connected to our bodhichitta, our awake heart, we long to offer something, anything. We may offer our wealth, our time, or our emotional support, but so long as it is a genuine offering from the heart we are making a difference on this earth.

The good news is that in our long journey to the other shore, the world will always provide us opportunities to offer ourselves. When we are confronted by someone requesting something from us, we can remember that generosity is a way to loosen our ego. In the words of Sakyong Mipham Rinpoche, "Holding on to anything is a way of holding on to ourselves."

## DISCIPLINE

Virtue and discipline go hand in hand. As was discussed in chapter 11, discipline is not about holding yourself to a fixed set of rules, but is based in holding your mind to the view of basic goodness.

The snow lion's discipline is rooted in the tiger's discernment. When we discover which aspects of our life bring about virtue and which bring about nonvirtue, the path of the snow lion is to stick to your guns and engage the acts that bring you joy. Often, these are acts that are based in virtue and compassion. For the bodhisattva who is training to work with obstacles, the discipline of being fully present and courageous with your heart is what leads you further down the spiritual path.

## PATIENCE

The snow lion is infinitely patient. Patience is something our parents told us to cultivate growing up. We never want to be patient; it's something not unlike discipline, which just seemed to be thrust upon us as a necessity of life.

Our conventional sense of patience is a "wait and see" approach. For example, we get a text message from our partner saying they "need to talk," and we have to be patient and wait until we see them in person to have a discussion. In the meantime, we sit there wondering if we are looking at good or bad news. We want to get this experience (whatever it may be) over with.

Patience from a Buddhist perspective is not a "wait and see" attitude, but rather one of "just be there." It is something we can take joy in cultivating. When you are sitting on the meditation cushion, a strong emotion, such as fear, might come up. You begin to think, "What if my presentation does not go well tomorrow?" That fear begins to creep up on you, growing as your mind starts to spiral into a variety of scenarios based in fear. Applying patience in this scenario is just being present with the emotion, letting it ebb and flow like the tide, while returning to your breath as much as possible.

Patience can also be based in not expecting anything. Think of patience as an act of being open to whatever comes your way. When you begin to solidify expectations, you get frustrated because they are never met in the way you had hoped. When you relax with whatever comes up without painting it with your own projections, then there is nothing to get impatient about. With no set idea of how something is supposed to be, it is hard to get stuck on things not happening in the time frame you desired. Instead, you are just being there, open to the possibilities of your life.

## JOYOUS EXERTION

As she leaps from mountaintop to mountaintop, the snow lion evades the trap of doubt with joyous exertion. At different points in our journey we may begin to fall into the trap of doubt, and start questioning what we're really doing practicing these qualities. We look at the beach behind us and say, "Maybe that wasn't so bad. Sure, it was sticky and dirty and people were pushy, but getting battered by the ocean isn't so great either." We begin to sink into laxity, and just let the waves bash us about.

When you are feeling lazy, it is just a sign that you should attempt to engage your world more fully. If your practice is starting to become less frequent, try doing some volunteer work or spending time with someone who could use support.

When you joyfully exert yourself for the sake of others, a natural perkiness occurs. You reconnect with your basic goodness and find further inspiration for your journey. Life no longer seems like such a hassle. Instead you can appreciate all the details of your world, including cooking your dinner, going to the movies with your friends, and paying your taxes. You can joyously exert yourself to be present with all these activities, grounding your experience in your own innate strength, your basic goodness.

## MEDITATION

The snow lion maintains meditative awareness in order to best see how she can be of benefit to others. It may seem obvious, but a bodhisattva works constantly with the mind of meditation as he meets the obstacles that come up in his life. You have become intimately familiar with your own emotional states on the meditation cushion. You know that clinging to a sense of self as real and solid only causes you more pain. The bodhisattva path entails letting go of those fixed notions, and instead tuning in to life as it is right now. Through constantly being present with your world, you have the opportunity to transform any adversity into an opportunity for practicing compassion.

## PRAJNA

These paramitas are all good on their own, but in order to employ them skillfully you need to follow the example of the snow lion and develop your own prajna, or "superior knowledge." *Pra* can be translated from Sanskrit as "super," and *jna* as "knowing." Prajna is thus superior knowledge, or to be a bit more verbose about it, discriminating-awareness wisdom. Prajna means that by applying discernment and great awareness, we can see things as they truly are.

Prajna is the quality of seeing a situation without painting your own projection onto it. It's removing the "me"-ness from a problem in order to see the best solution. When your own ego is not involved in determining the best course of action, you have removed the largest hindrance from seeing a situation as it is.

When you pay attention to a situation without coloring it with your set of opinions, the opportunity to do what is appropriate naturally arises. This is one of those "Come and see for yourself" moments in Buddhism. When you are next faced with an issue at work or among friends, step back a bit, drop your own opinion on the matter, and give the situation a lot of space. While resting in that space, see if a solution naturally dawns. At that moment, applying one of the previous paramitas might strike you as the best route forward.

The paramitas are transcendent because they are infused with prajna. Prajna is the intelligence that makes activities skillful. It is the knowledge that we have to drop our set point of view in order to gain a vaster idea of how to handle a situation.

I had an opportunity to see prajna in action one summer when I was living at Karmê Chöling, a retreat center in rural Vermont. It was a particularly busy summer, with several hundred people practicing meditation. Both the kitchen and the garden staff were working around-the-clock to make sure everyone got fed. Tension began to run high as people began to exhaust themselves.

One day a gentleman from the garden rushed across the lawn with a box full of tomatoes and ran into the kitchen. In his rush, he deposited the box right in the middle of someone's cooking station. Apparently this was not the first time this had happened.

As the garden worker scurried back to his job, the kitchen door flew open. The head chef had the box of tomatoes in his hands. Without saying a word, he threw the box after the garden worker. The box landed on its side on the ground, with tomatoes flying everywhere.

For a moment, everyone on the lawn was stunned to silence. The head chef glared at the garden worker. The garden worker glared back. After what seemed an eternity, each man turned around and stormed back to their work areas.

At that moment, a wave of opinion rose up. Some people began to talk about how inappropriate this was at a meditation center. Others thought mediation was required. Some thought one of the two men should be fired. Everyone had their own point of view on how things should proceed.

In the midst of this flurry of opinions, one young man stood up, and without saying a word, put the box right side up. He then picked up the tomatoes one by one, and placed them back in the box. He then placed the box away from the scene of the crime so it could be dealt with once the cloud of anger had passed.

I don't remember exactly what became of that particular argument. I doubt anyone does. What I do remember is that in the moment when everyone else immediately leaped forward to present their own point of view, one young man cut through the cloud of judgment by seeing the situation clearly. He knew that the kindest thing to do in that case was to check his ego at the door. Once he did that, he saw what no one else did: that the tomatoes should be picked up, and tempers should be allowed to cool. He offered space in the midst of confusion. This was the most compassionate thing that could have occurred.

Like this young man, we don't have to treat the paramitas as giant endeavors of good that need to be planned out. We don't have to become superheroes and fight evil at every turn. Instead, we can be present with our world, and offer help when the opportunity arises. It can be picking up a bottle off the sidewalk and placing it in a recycling bin, writing a check to a charity we wish to support, or just holding the elevator for someone.

When we lean in and embrace the paramitas, the waves of obstacles that present themselves no longer batter us around. We know how to work with these obstacles and utilize them as part of our journey. In fact, we relish the opportunity to apply generosity, discipline, patience, joyous exertion, meditation, and prajna. We know that by doing so we benefit others, but we also grow as a bodhisattva-in-training.

Through applying the six paramitas as much as possible, we navigate our samsaric existence with grace and dignity. These are the tools that all the enlightened masters of the past have honed through years of practice. If we follow in their footsteps, we too will be able to reach the other shore. Not unlike those realized masters, when we reach the shore of enlightenment and look back at everyone suffering, we are filled with a yearning to help them. These great meditation masters are said to then get back in the water and come back to the shore of suffering in an attempt to lead us all toward true awakening. It all begins with the six paramitas.

## CONTEMPLATION PRACTICE ON LOVING-KINDNESS

As a way to begin contemplating the paramitas, try this *maitri*, or loving-kindness, contemplation. Begin by sitting for a few minutes, practicing shamatha. Utilize this short meditation session as a chance to connect to your spacious being. By coming back to the breath over and over again, you are letting go of fixed ideas.

Within this space, first wish yourself true happiness. This does not need to be a big esoteric conundrum. You can make aspirations for simple things, like getting more sleep than you have lately, having a nice weekend, or enjoying your evening out with friends. At the very least, wish yourself a general sense of happiness. After a minute or two of offering yourself loving-kindness, think to yourself, "May I enjoy happiness and be free from suffering."

At this point, bring to mind someone you love. This could be your mother, your pet, a lover, or anyone who inspires a deep sense of adoration. Bring to mind their image, some quality about them that you enjoy, or even just their name. Then wish them happiness in as specific terms as you can muster. You can think to yourself, "May Will get that job offer" or "I hope Mom has a happy birthday." If nothing specific comes to mind, just wish that individual a general sense of happiness, health, and well-being. After a few minutes, conclude this section by saying, "May that person [use their name] enjoy happiness and be free from suffering."

Try to do the same thing with a friend of yours. This can be someone who cheers you up when times get down, or just someone you see once in a blue moon for a beer. Think of this friend and what they are working with in their life. Wish them success and happiness, focusing on that for a few minutes. Then end this section of the contemplation by thinking, "May they enjoy happiness and be free from suffering."

Now bring to mind someone you don't know as well, but who you see regularly. This could be the person who runs your local Laundromat, a classmate, a postal worker, or anyone who you don't really have extreme feelings about. Because you don't know them very well, you aren't kept up late at night worrying about the issues in their life. While you may not know much about them, try wishing them happiness. Know that they want to be happy, just like you. After a couple of minutes, say to yourself, "May they enjoy happiness and be free from suffering."

Bring to mind someone who you genuinely dislike. Traditionally this is referred to as your enemy. Assuming you have not accumulated an archnemesis, I recommend you bring to mind someone you just can't seem to get along with. Even if strong emotions come up around this person, try to wish them happiness in whatever form you feel comfortable with. This could be specific, such as hoping they do well in an athletic endeavor, or find happiness with a new partner. After a few minutes of working with this person, conclude by saying, "May they enjoy happiness and be free from suffering."

At this point, let the loving-kindness grow big enough to include all the beings that you have just contemplated. Do not consider some of them friends and others enemies, but dissolve the boundaries of opinion and wish them happiness as a group: "May they enjoy happiness and be free from suffering." Rest in that feeling for a minute or two.

From there, extend loving-kindness even further. Without discrimination, offer the emotion you have been working with to all beings. You can start close to home, in your neighborhood, wishing happiness for everyone on your block. Then go further, offering happiness and freedom from suffering to everyone in your town or city, your state, your country, and so on, until your loving-kindness is offered to the entire world. You can think to yourself, or even express out loud, "May all beings enjoy happiness and the root of happiness."

Be present with whatever comes from this contemplation. Dropping the specific words, relax with the meaning of this aspiration and the experience of love. Let love fill your heart to the point that it spills out and radiates to all beings. Rest your mind in that state.

You can engage this practice regularly as a way to encourage yourself to extend your heart to others. If you practice this loving-kindness contemplation in the morning, it can snap you out of any hesitation you may have about engaging in the practices of a bodhisattva.

Then at the end of the day, you can reflect on how much you engaged in wishing others happiness, and how much you practiced applying the six paramitas to your life. This is not a chance for judgment; if you sense you did not work much with these principles during the day, let that simply fuel your desire to do more the next day. If you find you have applied loving-kindness and compassion practices to your day, you should celebrate in whatever way feels appropriate to you.

# 13 / BRINGING LIGHT TO A DARK WORLD

At some point in our spiritual path, it's no longer just about us. It's about making a difference in this world. We have a very simple choice: we can get overwhelmed by the rampant desire, aggression, and ignorance that surround us, or we can face it head-on.

We can apply the snow lion's discipline to go beyond our habitual routine, and face difficult situations with compassion, the discipline of virtue, and the six paramitas. If we go this route, we are bringing radiance to even the darkest corners of our world. Let's explore how we can apply the snow lion's tools to major areas of our life: our 9 to 5, our family, our money, volunteering, and compassionate leadership.

## Our 9 to 5

The snow lion knows that everyone she encounters in her day is worthy of her compassion. Most of us spend the majority of our waking hours surrounded by people we would not necessarily choose as company. They are our coworkers, bosses, classmates, or professors. Some of them are annoying, others are constantly anxious, while others are just infuriating. We can't spend all our time at work or school daydreaming about when we are going to be free from these people. If we want to be true warriors in the world, we need to ground ourselves in our present situation and apply our compassionate activity to these tough individuals.

It might be helpful to keep a list of the six paramitas on your desk. I recommend writing each one out nicely on a card, and keeping those cards sitting on a stand in front of you. When you answer the phone and someone starts ranting and raving about how you should have done a task differently, you might feel inclined to cut them off or correct them. Imagine what a blessing it would be at that moment if your eyes happened to fall on the single word *patience*. The other person could ramble on and exhaust themselves while you took the dignified high road by applying this paramita.

I guarantee that at least one paramita will apply to whatever you encounter during your 9 to 5. You can apply generosity by covering a coworker's lunch when they are short on cash and looking longingly at your sandwich. When a meeting is spiraling out of control, you can tune in to meditative mind and bring the conversation back down to earth. Whenever you are faced with an intense work situation, scroll through the six paramitas in your mind and see how creatively you can apply each of these tools.

## OUR FAMILY

Our family life can be an excellent training ground for spiritual practice. For example, there comes a time in any young person's life when they realize that their parents simply do not have it all together. Yes, your mother or father may have a solid job, manage to stay married, and even keep their cholesterol at a tolerable level. At the same time, I am guessing your mom or dad would be the first to admit that they do not have their lives all planned out. They had no guidebook when raising you or figuring out their career, and that means you won't be inheriting that manual. This realization can lead to heartbreak, confusion, and disappointment.

The path of the snow lion is to not give in to this particular brand of doubt. At a certain point, the relationship between child and parent shifts. You don't have to be horrified that your parents aren't perfectly together beings; you can relish it. This realization can open the doors for compassion to flourish. Instead of shying away from tough family issues, you apply the discipline of virtue by leaning in and opening up a dialogue about them. Your communication can become a two-way street so both you and your family members can learn more about one another. Part of showing our family members compassion (all of them, not just our parents) involves being willing to listen to them even as they go into topics that are potentially painful for both of you.

We know experientially that our life falls apart in a million ways all the time. Whatever illusion of security we think we can find in external circumstances can vanish in a moment's time. The most precious people to us, our family members, experience the same thing. As painful as it is to see them struggle, there are times when the most compassionate thing we can do is be fully present with them as they work through these challenges. Offering our support even when it is tough to do so is the act of a bodhisattva.

## Our Money

In chapter 7, we explored how to apply the qualities of the tiger to enter into a healthy relationship with money. But treating money as part of our spiritual path is not just about our personal relationship with wealth. Whenever we use money, it puts us in a relationship with others. Looking to the paramitas of generosity and discipline, we can investigate how money affects the world around us. If we use money correctly, we can realize the traditional Buddhist saying, "Generosity is the virtue that produces peace."

Using the tiger's discernment, we see how money can be spent in a way we feel good about (a nice birthday gift for a friend), as well as ways we feel less pleased about (an expensive video game bought on impulse, which leaves our wallet empty when it comes time to take our niece out to lunch). We begin to see which spending patterns make us happy and which bring us pain.

From there we can apply the discipline of the snow lion to follow through on our discernment. If we discover that we enjoy sponsoring an impoverished child overseas, then the discipline of the snow lion is to follow through and make a real connection with that individual or increase our level of giving. If we see we do not like overpaying for groceries, the discipline of the snow lion is going a bit farther outside our neighborhood for a cheaper grocer that we enjoy.

Some people may be interested in investing their money. Knowing that the way we spend our money has an effect on the world around us, we have to be careful about where it goes. You may have the chance to make a decision between investing in something that will yield the largest return and something that causes the least harm. These decisions matter because they are not just based in your personal financial well-being, but in our global economy, which means they affect people across the world.

You may also find great joy in offering money to charity. Giving just a little more than what you might normally feel comfortable offering allows you to build up your generosity muscles. Not only are you making a difference in the world, but this also allows you to grow as a person. You see money as a tool to bring benefit to the world. You no longer have to view money in terms of a "me versus the world" scenario, but you can use it to uplift both the world and yourself.

## VOLUNTEERING

In my opinion, the simplest way to engage the path of a bodhisattva is to volunteer. When you bring your meditative practice to the neglected areas of your community, it is like bringing a lantern into a dark cave. Your open heart radiates out, touching everyone directly.

I recently read that one of the top New Year resolutions in the United States is to volunteer more. This is a very general aspiration, like spending more time with family and friends, but it shows up year after year on this list. As a nation, it appears that Americans want to help. We just don't often cut through our habitual routine long enough to do it.

A few years back my teacher, Sakyong Mipham Rinpoche, requested that his students take on a formal volunteer post. I myself ended up having dinner with a friend who worked in hospice care, and before I knew it I was an active hospice volunteer, spending time with three elderly individuals who had entered the dying process.

All three of these elders were too far gone for me to develop a long-term relationship with them. The most I could do was offer my presence. This meant many hours of just being a steady presence while they were asleep, or talking with them about wherever their minds went when they were awake. It was not complicated or time-consuming. It was actually refreshing in how simple and straightforward it was. I just had to offer myself, and was met without judgment.

Despite the lack of depth in our conversations, I felt close to all of them, and whenever one of them passed away, I was very sad. Without realizing it, these relationships touched me deeply. While I may have thought I was offering a service to them, I learned a great deal by understanding a bit about their lives and watching them as they struggled with old age and death.

When you take on a formal volunteer commitment, it can change you for life. It can teach you valuable lessons while softening your very being. If you cannot commit to a formal volunteer role, consider how you can take time out to care for others in your daily life. The snow lion knows that making time for others makes the world a bit brighter, and can be as refreshing as a crisp fall morning.

## COMPASSIONATE LEADERSHIP

The other week I was teaching a meditation class, and a student mentioned that she felt disheartened by the sheer number of, in her words, "corporate douche bags" that held leadership positions in the world's largest companies. "Where," she asked, "are the role models for us to follow in being moral citizens in the workplace?"

There is no simple answer to this question, perhaps because our corporate role models are few and far between. That is why many of my own role models are leaders in noncorporate fields. Still, if we work in a corporate setting or any place where greed is rewarded, it is up to us to employ Mahatma Gandhi's maxim, "Be the change you want to see in the world."

If we begin to lead by example, practicing compassion, the discipline of virtue, and the six paramitas in our offices, schools, and parties, people will pick up on that. These principles of the snow lion are extremely attractive. They are rare in today's world, and as a result they are easily recognizable. Without necessarily longing to be in a leadership position, people will be magnetized to you, asking your advice and looking for guidance.

By merely practicing opening your heart on a daily basis, you may get pegged by people as someone worthy of respect. You can reverse the current culture based on putting yourself before all others. You do not have to be a corporate douche bag to get ahead. Instead you can model a new openhearted style of leadership. You yourself can be the role model for how to lead effectively and in a compassionate matter.

There are an infinite number of ways we can apply the qualities of the snow lion to our path of warriorship. The above are merely suggestions for how you can apply compassion, the discipline of virtue, and the six paramitas to the world around you. The more you lean into your world and engage it, the more you will see opportunities to employ these qualities of the snow lion.

In order to skillfully make obstacles your path, you must develop faith in your basic goodness and be willing to offer bodhichitta every day of your life. That generator of compassionate activity illuminates obstacles and makes them workable. The beauty of these teachings is that by bringing bodhichitta to all aspects of your life, you are not only offering compassion to others, but you will find true joy in yourself.

The world is hungry for these qualities of mindfulness and compassion. It needs a new generation of leaders who aspire for a culture based in empathy and wisdom. We can be those leaders. We can create an enlightened society. We can help transform the world with the power of an open heart.

## Part Three

# LETTING GO INTO SPACE

# 14 / PLUCK THE ARROW FROM YOUR EYE AND SEE THE WORLD MORE CLEARLY

I had a drink with a friend the other night. He is going through a rough breakup, and was doing that thing we all do when going through a breakup: trying to identify the causes and conditions that led to the relationship's demise. At one point he looked up from his beer and came to the conclusion, "I just expected too much from her. And she from me."

In some sense, he said, each party had wanted something from the other that they were not willing to give. Each of them also expected the other to change over time in order to accommodate those expectations. As my friend came to find out, whenever we set expectations down in stone like this, we are sure to end up disappointed.

This basic principle is true not just for romantic relationships, but for any aspect of our life. For some people, going home to visit their parents is the rough equivalent of regressing to their teenage self. You expect to enter your childhood house as an adult, but old ideas have hung around the home front, and instead of talking politics and movies you find yourself taking out the trash, raking leaves, and getting into decade-old fights with your folks. This level of expectation is not what you signed on for, but it tends to rear its head over and over again in different forms. Expectation is a nasty beast, one that tends to ensnare us all.

## The Arrows of Passion, Aggression, and Ignorance

When we take a look at expectation, we see two major factors at play: hope and fear. We hope to find happiness at a new position at work, but fear that we will be surrounded by the same corporate mentality we have come to despise. We hope to get a nice birthday gift. We fear the scary neighborhood on our commute home. No matter the scenario, we long for pleasure and shy away from potential pain. For just about everyone, our whole existence is governed by these simple reactions.

There is a traditional image of samsara that is quite popular. Formally known as the twelve links of causation, it describes twelve pieces that come together to form the solid sense of "me" that we all carry around throughout our life. One of those links depicts a man with an arrow in his eye.

As gruesome as this sounds, I sort of like this image. This gentleman with an arrow stuck in his eye represents the way we develop feelings about our world. When you perceive something, be it a piece of cake or a potential new career path, it is likely you have one of three basic reactions, based on hope and fear. You might desire it, and engage in actively wanting and longing for it. You might aggressively distance yourself from it, despising the very notion and fighting against it. Or you might just want to ignore it, hoping it will go away. Whatever comes up in your life, you can contemplate how quickly you might tend to leap to these three reactions of passion, aggression, and ignorance.

Our man with an arrow in his eye is no different from you or me. He wants to be happy. However, he has this arrow stuck in him and it hurts. So he's constantly fiddling with it. He thinks, "If I can move it a bit to the right, I won't be in pain. No, that didn't work! I'll just try and wiggle it around to the left. Ouch. OK, I'll just shove it in a bit more and see if that helps." He continues to seek only pleasure, and longs to rid himself of pain, yet no matter what he does he can't ease his suffering.

If you are constantly solidifying strong opinions and expectations, it is just as if you are sticking an arrow in your eye. It is foolish to think that we will find lasting happiness by trying to change things to make them more in line with our desires. For example, Alex hated commuting by public transportation, so he got a new car. As we took a ride together in the car, he said it was really great, but he wanted to get a better sound system. He got the sound system, but a few months later he began to complain about how quickly the car went through gas. It went on like that until the car started breaking down. Now, he refers to the car as a "money pit" that drains his bank account and brings him no pleasure. This new car is one of many arrows in my friend's eye.

We have spent our whole life fiddling with our own personal arrows. Until we begin to cut through stuck expectations about how we think things ought to be, we are likely going to keep fiddling with these arrows, causing ourselves more pain in the pursuit of greater pleasure.

In the second section, we looked at aspiring to follow the path of the Mahayana, or greater vehicle. The snow lion is one aspect of the Mahayana. She represents the relative Mahayana where we learn to develop compassion for others in order to be of benefit to the world. This is an extremely important aspect of our spiritual path.

However, if you truly want to be of benefit but your head is full of stuck expectations about how the world should be, you will only go out and spread those fixed opinions. It is like offering advice to someone who hasn't yet told you about their problem: it doesn't work because you are putting the cart before the horse. In the same way, if you do not perceive reality correctly, you may think you are doing the most compassionate thing possible, but it's just your personal view of compassion, and this may or may not mesh with others' perspectives.

This is where the absolute perspective of the Mahayana path is helpful. This aspect of the Mahayana journey looks directly at reality and how we perceive it. Currently, you likely experience yourself as a solid self—a fixed "me" with certain opinions and ways of doing things. Sometimes the world around you supports what you want to do, but other times you feel buffered around by the world like a beach ball at a Dave Matthews Band concert.

From our discussion in previous chapters, you know (at least on a conceptual level) that this solid sense of "me" shifts all the time. You know that the world around you changes constantly as well. Armed with this knowledge, you have a choice. You can fight samsara. This is a road you have walked down your entire life. It leads to getting thrown around like that beach ball. Alternatively, you can let go of fixed points of view and perceive your world without laying your personal trip on top of it. Even though it seems counter to what you may normally do, letting go of our fixed view is like plucking the arrow from your eye and walking carefree through your world.

Your meditation practice is based in cutting through your fixed point of view and your personal trip, so you're already on your way to plucking out the arrow and loosening up that solid sense of self. You are engaged in a spiritual journey that vehemently attacks the solid "me" by ripping into habitual patterns on and off the cushion. Furthermore, the practices of meditation and offering yourself to others have shifted your focus away from "me." It is at this point that you can look to the absolute Mahayana path, which is based in deconstructing the duality of "me" and "other" and truly resting in your basic goodness.

## VIPASHYANA: THE NEXT STEP ON THE JOURNEY

There is a meditation experience within which we can examine this duality we have created of "me" and "other." It is known as *vipashyana*. The Sanskrit word *vipashyana* can be translated as "superior seeing." It is known as superior seeing because we are looking at our world without layering "me" and "my opinions" on top of it.

Imagine wearing a pair of really nice designer sunglasses. Your particular glasses have these very fancy lenses that shift from passion to aggression to ignorance, depending on what you are looking at. However, if you can rest in the present moment, it is as if your glasses suddenly have clear lenses: you are wearing normal glasses that help you see your world. You are seeing the world in a superior way; seeing it clearly as a bright and vibrant place.

We have previously considered shamatha practice as the means to be present with our world. Vipashyana takes being present to the next level by saying, "OK, now that you're here and seeing things correctly, let's examine what it is you're seeing." It is the idea that on and off the meditation cushion we are not just being in the moment, but we are also investigating the nature of that moment itself. We are entering into the absolute Mahayana perspective by learning to examine samsara.

Don't worry if you have not consciously applied vipashyana before. As you continue to deepen your meditation practice, you may find that this happens quite naturally. Before you were just trying to stay with the breath, but now when you meditate, you often feel like you have developed further insight into who you are. Furthermore, you are starting to see the transient nature of the world around you, how ephemeral your thoughts really are, and you are having an easier time noticing when you are about to get hooked by a habitual emotional reaction. This is vipashyana starting to inform your point of view.

After your next meditation session, take the following hour to notice how vipashyana manifests in your life. As you prepare to go to work, feed your pets, or do any of your normal activities, notice your initial reactions as they come up. Do you feel attracted to certain things? Are there things you are immediately repulsed by? Are there times when you just shut down and ignore something? Take a nonjudgmental stance and just notice how these three root reactions manifest in your daily life. At the end of the hour, notice how your vipashyana practice has affected your degree of insight and your experience of daily activities.

Thus far we have been training in being in this moment, right now. Going forward we need to learn to investigate "right now." We need to contemplate the nature of right now. When we do, we may find that this moment is not as frozen or solid as it might have initially seemed. We can begin to relax into it without strong concepts or assumptions. This is an essential step on our journey.

We are exploring the Mahayana path not just as altruistic men or women, but we are starting to see that we can play with the space and uncomfortable aspects of our lives. The world around us is inherently impermanent and constantly changing. We can rejoice in that knowledge and relax our expectations. We can start to move beyond our set of hopes and fears.

This next step on our Mahayana path can seem scary. When we first sat down to learn about meditation, it may simply have been because we wanted to relax. Maybe we were OK with the relative aspect of the Mahayana and enjoyed doing good deeds and offering our heart to others. Now we are being asked to step into groundless territory, and explore the nature of reality itself. We are beginning to examine our "self," an idea that might appear to present a Pandora's box of philosophical issues.

As we move forward on our path, we need to continue to reflect on the qualities of gentleness that the tiger embodies, as well as to notice when we fall into the trap of doubt so that we can apply the perkiness of the snow lion. Remembering the qualities of the tiger and snow lion, we are well armed to begin examining our set notion of "me," as well as this other thing that excites or terrifies us called "everything that is not me," that is to say, our world.

## Examining the Self

Throughout history, when people have discussed notions of "self," they have developed a tendency to fall into extreme points of view. There are many schools of thought that consider the self as something permanent. This is referred to as eternalism, the idea that beings are born, age, and die, but ultimately contain some essence that lasts forever.

When I was in college, the brother of a close friend died in a drunk-driving accident. Sean was seventeen when he passed away, and his family and friends were devastated, as you would imagine. I spent a good amount of time with Sean's family during that period of time. In the weeks that followed his death, an idea arose in the family's community of support that Sean had been called up to God to be one of his angels. While none of us could explain logically why such a death would befall a good kid like Sean, it was reassuring to think he had been called to heaven for a higher purpose.

I have no qualms about anyone believing in God, heaven, or angels. In fact, I was heartened to see how this idea helped Sean's family during a time of intense grief. However, for my own sake, I began contemplating the nature of these ideas. I began applying vipashyana. I heeded the words of the Buddha when he instructed, "Come and see for yourself," and I began to see what I could and could not prove about this idea using my own experience.

Upon examining the idea, I found that I could not definitively prove that there was a god that called Sean to heaven. I also could not prove that there was anything solid that would leave Sean's body and go anywhere really. When I looked at my experience, I saw that I could not find anything in the world around me that was permanent at all. Thus I personally could not subscribe to this eternalistic point of view. In my exploration of this tragedy, I could only find proof of one thing, which was the opposite of the eternalistic view: that Sean's death was another reminder of impermanence.

Nihilism is another popular way of considering the self. This extreme point of view is a bit fatalistic. Nihilism in a traditional sense is the complete opposite of eternalism. A nihilist would say that absolutely nothing survives after we die. Our body is dead, and that's that. As a result, there are some nihilists who believe it's OK to ignore all the suffering in the world and just party all the time.

People who subscribe to nihilism can shrug their shoulders at the world, thinking that there is some universal plan which they cannot impact in any way. Have you ever had coffee with someone, and in an offhand way they say, "I'm just supposed to be single right now; that's my karma"? It's as if they believe they cannot go to a bar, post a profile on a dating website, or make any effort to meet someone. You don't need to have a lot of meditative insight to know that this is not the case. It seems silly to live your life in a nihilistic fashion, thinking that you have no control over anything.

While seemingly contradictory, eternalism and nihilism do meet at one point. Both schools of thought believe in a solid "self." Eternalism believes that you have a "self" that continues on after this body is dead. Nihilism believes that you have a "self" that exists in this place and time, and that's really all you have.

The Buddhist point of view departs from both of these schools, and claims that there is no substantial "self" at all. If we examine our reality, we see that eternalism and nihilism represent extreme versions of hope and fear. There is the extreme hope that we will live forever in some form, and there is the extreme fear that we will perish no matter what. The Buddhist notion is to not buy into either hope or fear, and instead know the self to be illusory, empty of solid substance. When we cut through extreme hope and fear, we can touch our own innate wisdom.

## The Outrageous Garuda

In this section we will explore the outrageous garuda. Half-man, half-bird, the garuda flies through the air, shrieking out the reality of our existence. The garuda is outrageous because while doing so he flies above petty concerns, rivalries, and klesha activity. In fact, the garuda is not caught up in "me" at all.

The garuda applies vipashyana to whatever he encounters. He does what we long to do: he accepts whatever comes up in his life and rolls with whatever winds come his way. He addresses situations with clear perception, having removed his "me"-tinged glasses, and no longer is overwhelmed by hope and fear, or passion, aggression, and ignorance. To return to the traditional image of the twelve links of causation, the garuda has plucked the arrow from his eye.

As we begin to examine our sense of "self" and the world around us, we enter into the absolute Mahayana path, encountering reality without that arrow lodged in our eye. We start to see how passion, aggression, and ignorance lead us to extreme beliefs or concepts, aspects of our mind that take us away from reality.

We need to relax our concepts about who we think we are, what the world should be like, and how we think we ought to be treated. Part of this exploration will be examining the fluid and impermanent quality of our lives. Like the garuda, we can rejoice in the simple truths of our reality and, from there, experience equanimity. We can scrub away at our tendency to only fixate on "me" and instead focus on the world as the rich and beautiful place it truly is.

# 15 / THE FEARLESS FLIGHT
## OF THE GARUDA

Have you ever had a dream in which you could fly? It's a very liberating feeling. If I realize during a dream that I am in fact dreaming, I suddenly say to myself, "Hey, I'm not bound by conventional rules, I might as well make the most of it." From there I take off and soar fearlessly into space.

It is said that many great meditation masters throughout history have mastered the art of flight. One example is the Tibetan yogi Milarepa, who as a result of his meditative absorption, attained the level of accomplishment, or *siddhi*, which allowed him to fly in real life.

You can buy into this sort of story or not, as you like. The basic idea behind it, though, is that through intensive training, anyone can soar through their life, at least metaphorically. We utilize our meditation training to loosen our concepts about what is and is not possible, which in turn makes us feel like we are walking on air.

In the first two sections, we looked at earthbound animals. The tiger meticulously walks through the jungle. He is very rooted in his environment and takes great care as he engages everyday acts. The snow lion leaps about from mountaintop to mountaintop. She feels great buoyancy because she is not caught in the trap of doubt, but she too has to eventually make a home back on earth.

Going forward, we look to the example of the mythical garuda. We are leaving the solidity of earth behind us by looking to a bird that is not your typical backyard robin. I am guessing you have never seen a garuda in person before. I have not either. The very act of visualizing it challenges our concepts of how we think things should be.

Even though we cannot go on safari and point at a garuda, we can still visualize this mythical bird. It is said to have a large body with a sharp beak and human arms. The garuda is born in space, and as such he is ready to fly from the moment of birth. He never lands on the ground, but continuously flies above his world. From that vantage point, he maintains a bird's-eye view of his surroundings.

The garuda is not attached to a formal sense of "me," and as a result, he is able to expand his view. When you study the example of the tiger, you learn how to take a look at your own life. As you engage the path of the snow lion, you begin to expand your vision to include people you like, people you feel neutral toward, and people you have a hard time with. In the loving-kindness contemplation described in chapter 12, we end by dissolving the boundaries between those individuals and offering our practice to everyone. The garuda starts at this last point: having cut through only thinking about "me," he is able to continuously offer himself to all beings.

The garuda soars high above the earth. As a result, friends and enemies look like ants to him. He cannot distinguish between them, nor does he want to. Instead, he envelops all of them with the same level of compassionate activity. The garuda is beyond any fixed concepts about what he can or cannot do, or who he can or cannot give his support to. He fearlessly offers his heart to all, without worrying about what people will think of him.

## RECOGNIZING THE NATURE OF FEAR

It is said that the garuda evades the trap of falling into hope and fear. Yet when you think about it, hope is just an inversion of fear. When you say, "I hope I get to work on time," you are really just saying, "I'm worried I'll be late." When you hope that your lover feels as strongly as you do, it's actually a concern that they very well may not. When you see an e-mail in your in-box and hope it's the good news you're expecting, part of you believes that it will actually be bad news. If we apply an inquisitive eye to hope, we see that it is directly linked to fear. So instead of saying the garuda is free from the trap of hope and fear, we can simplify this and say that he is fearless.

*Fearless* is an interesting term when considered from a Shambhala Buddhist point of view. On first read, it might seem that the garuda has mastered fear itself, and that he is experiencing less fear than before. This is not the case. There will always be things in the world that cause fear. I don't think that at any point in the history of Buddhism someone invented some philosophy or device to reduce the causes of fear in the world. If so, that person's latest reincarnation should be found, and hired to work for the United Nations.

All of us have our own triggers for fear. If you have been in a car accident, you might be jumpy getting into a taxicab. If you have had a bad experience with heights, you may be scared of being in tall buildings or amusement park rides. If you have ever seen an older relative's body or mind deteriorate over time, you might have a fear of old age. Perhaps you fear all of the above.

Everyone experiences fear, even the great Buddhist masters. Fear is an emotional state, and since these teachers are human, they feel it just as much as you or me. In fact, they feel it just as potently as they do love, jealousy, or desire. They simply do not get hooked by the strong emotion like we are prone to do.

Similarly, the garuda experiences fear. However, because the garuda is a master warrior, he does not get hooked by fear. This is why we say that the garuda is fearless. He sees fear, then he recognizes the nature of fear, and he soars headfirst into it, coming out unhooked and as refreshed as if he just took a long shower. The garuda is able to navigate fear so easily because he knows that the world is a fluid, changing entity. He does not bother solidifying his opinions about the world because he knows it will change. Without set expectations about how things should be, he can greet fear, embrace it, and make friends with that emotion.

Fearlessness in the Shambhala tradition is about working with the emotion of fear as it arises. It is about being present with fear when we feel it stuck in our mind. It is about examining fear fully, and trying to deconstruct it. It is not about having less fear, but about entering into a gentle process of understanding fear and, as a result, using fear as an opportunity to progress on a spiritual path.

When fear arises, our job is to welcome it like an old friend, one who is back to visit your home after many years away. We greet fear and try to learn as much about it as we can while it visits, knowing that at some point fear will indeed depart. When we lean into fear this way, we follow the example of the garuda. We can see the ephemeral and impermanent nature of fear more clearly, and ultimately we can rest in its presence.

## THE BASIC TRUTHS OF THE GARUDA

There are a number of basic truths the garuda acknowledges as part of its path of working through fear and relaxing into spacious wisdom: impermanence, groundlessness, and equanimity. We will be delving deeper into these three topics in the next three chapters.

### IMPERMANENCE

Impermanence is a hard truth to deny. Even if you sit in one place and try to make nothing change, the world around you shifts constantly. Perhaps like me, you enjoy gazing out your window in the morning, particularly on beautiful autumn days. But even though the scene outside is lovely, it's hard to ignore that the vivid colors are fading, and the leaves are falling on the ground. After a few autumns have come and gone, you do not need a degree in rocket science to know that years have passed you by. In that process, your own body ages, as do those of your friends and relatives. Just by gazing outside in the morning, we are faced with the simple truth that things age and change.

For example, you are not the same person you were ten years ago. Let's contemplate that simple idea to see what we can find. Next time you are able to practice meditation, take some time to rest in shamatha. After sitting for a few minutes, contemplate the question, "What was I like ten years ago?" Contemplate what sort of things you were doing this month, ten years prior. If you can't remember specifics, try to get a general feel for it. Were you in school? Working? Were you romantically involved with someone? What activities and hobbies were you pursuing then?

Now contemplate what has changed since that time. You don't have to tease out all the different threads, such as whether you are still collecting stamps. Simply contemplate, "Am I that same person?" You will likely find that there are aspects about that person that you still embody, but nonetheless a good deal has shifted over a decade.

When you have spent five minutes contemplating the amount of change that has taken place over ten years, practice shamatha once more before ending your session.

From a scientific point of view, every cell in your body dies and is replaced over a period of seven years. This means that even if you are working at the same job, drinking the same brand of coffee every morning, living with the same partner, fighting the same habitual fights with that person, after seven years you still end up in a brand-new body. We could live a very cloistered existence and try to hide from the truth of change, but it will always find us.

Just because impermanence surrounds us, it doesn't mean that change has to be a bad or scary thing. There are times when impermanence may feel like a blessing, such as when you have the flu and you eventually get better. There may be someone in your life that you previously had a hard time with, then circumstances shifted around your relationship and today he or she is one of your closest friends. At one point your apartment felt lonely, but now you have a live-in partner or a pet that brightens your day. Change can be refreshing at times.

Change happens to everyone. Often it is easy to see change in yourself, but harder to see it in the people around you. For example, I think my mother looks the same as she did fifteen years ago. Others might disagree and say I am just not acknowledging change. I don't think I'm alone in having a hard time acknowledging my parents' aging process. No one likes to see that their parents are getting older. Still, this change is undeniable, and we are forced to work with this and many other reminders of impermanence.

One aspect of impermanence is death. Sakyong Mipham Rinpoche wrote a meditation practice intended for birthdays. One line reads, "Death is my friend, the truest of friends, a true friend that never abandons me." It might seem morbid to contemplate death on one's birthday. However, when you think about it, death is a part of life. Reminding ourselves of death is what allows us to live our life to the fullest, and to take advantage of the time we do have on this earth. As a result, death is a friend because he reminds us of the preciousness of life.

The garuda embraces these truths of impermanence and death. He does not dwell on them, constantly worrying about losing his feathers or getting hit by a plane. Instead, he utilizes this knowledge to be sure that he makes the most of his life and the relationships he encounters, and spends his time attempting to be of benefit to all.

## GROUNDLESSNESS

Knowing that everything around us is subject to change could lead to anxiety. Even though you know that a romantic relationship is impermanent, the idea that your partner might leave you—or worse, die—is scary business. When the relationship actually ends, you feel like the proverbial rug has been pulled out from under you. Up is down, right is left, and you're not sure what is going on. In other words, you feel groundless.

It is only natural to feel groundless when faced with sudden change. For some people, getting fired makes them feel like the world is crumbling around them. For others, it's when a relationship is cut off prematurely or ends on bad terms. And for others, it is getting sick and watching their body degenerate. The fact that we feel groundless at times is inevitable; it is based in the truth of impermanence.

How we work with groundlessness is an important part of the path of the garuda. If we look to his example, we see that the garuda does not cling to the strong emotions that come with groundlessness. If the garuda loses his job, he doesn't panic and say, "Oh my God! I'm destitute!" He flies headfirst into the emotional upheaval and addresses it in a less chaotic, more straightforward manner. Instead of tightening up, he relaxes. He sorts out the details of his life in a dignified way. He continues to soar because he has not been lassoed down to earth by buying into fear.

## EQUANIMITY

As a result of working intimately with all the impermanence and the groundlessness he encounters in the world, the garuda develops the next truth, equanimity.

Through looking clearly at the parts of our life that scare us, we are learning to let go. We are letting go of maintaining this solid "me" that has to have things a certain way. Like the garuda, we are engaging a path of riding the energy of our life. Instead of getting hooked by fear, or by how we think things ought to be, we can face whatever comes up with an unbiased attitude. We can face the world with equanimity.

If we think of the image of the garuda soaring in space, it's hard to imagine him having a really panicked look on his face. He is above trivial concerns like anxiety or pride. He is not looking for a security blanket to wrap himself up in. He is not shielding his heart from the world. He is not building a cocoon of fear to hide behind. He manifests a sense of freedom and openness.

When we follow in the example of the garuda, we too do not buy into hope and fear, and as a result, we are free to perceive our world clearly. We see the problems that face us, and we address them in just as straightforward a manner as the garuda. We do not see impermanence and groundlessness as problems, but instead as opportunities to practice maintaining an open heart. By continuing to be fearless in the face of adversity, we find true peace and equanimity.

# 16 / STUDYING FOR YOUR BUDDHIST BAR MITZVAH

When you're finished changing, you're finished.

—*Benjamin Franklin*

Prince Siddhartha was raised in a manner in which all suffering was hidden away from him. Change to him was always positive. His father ensured that it was a new dancing girl coming to his palace, or a comfier bed to sleep on. When the people who lived in his palace began to age recognizably, they were removed. If anyone became ill, they disappeared until they grew well again. If someone he knew happened to die, he was never told of their passing.

Imagine living a life where you truly had no knowledge of aging, sickness, or death. Think of the amount of energy that went into manufacturing the illusion that these basic aspects of our existence don't exist at all. Now consider how shocking it must have been for our friend Sid when he was in his twenties and he finally encountered these simple truths. No one had ever told him that he himself would feel the pains of old age and eventually die! He was shaken to his core, and these truths inspired him to pursue his spiritual journey.

To many of us, this story may seem outlandish. How can anyone truly not know about aging, sickness, and death? Yet if you look carefully, you will see that our current society tries to replicate the exact same illusion that took place in Siddhartha's palace. We have multibillion-dollar industries devoted to modifying people's appearances so they appear pleasing. If you are young, there is makeup that will make you appear older. If you are beginning to show marks of aging, there is surgery that will take away your wrinkles. If you are very old, you may be placed in an "old age home" that is not your home, where you will be sequestered until you die. That is how scared we are of impermanence and death.

## EVEN CELL PHONES DIE

Obviously, no one likes to spend their day dwelling on the fact that they will grow old and die. It's not pleasant for us. However, we have to acknowledge and explore these aspects of our life if we want to work through our fears and encounter reality in a straightforward manner. If we are going to follow in the path of the garuda, we must be willing to look at things as they are. We can take any factor in our life and can examine it in order to find that it is transient, changing, and impermanent.

For example, you might believe that a new phone will make you happy. It is supposed to free up time in your life by allowing you to check e-mail while you're on the go. The next thing you know, your relationship to e-mail has changed. You are constantly checking your phone in a panic, wondering what is going on at work. If you work in an office building, watch your colleagues when they get in the elevator. Presumably they are all on their way to their jobs, but many people will take out their phones and check their e-mail, already fearing what the day might bring. They cannot rest in the space of a thirty-second elevator ride without anxiety overriding their experience and urging them to fiddle with their phones. What we thought would bring us happiness is just allowing us to freak out about work on a more regular basis.

Eventually that new phone that you thought would bring you happiness slips out of your hand and breaks on the floor. The colloquial expression for this loss is having your cell phone "die." It is as if your phone was a living person, one that you cannot do without. The funny thing is that by this point, you actually feel like you can't live without your phone. You get another phone and use it to send an e-mail to all of your friends saying, "Help! I lost your number because my cell phone died." Just as if you had experienced a true death in your family, people write you condolence notes.

Somewhere in this messy process, we need to lighten up and see how ludicrous this whole affair is. An object you thought would bring you more freedom has in fact limited you, and it has become another source of anxiety in your life. Your phone cannot bring you everlasting joy; it's absurd to think this piece of metal and buttons and wires ever could. It is subject to the laws of impermanence, and falls apart just like everything else.

We can either cling tightly to our world by thinking that external factors (including people) will be able to bring us true happiness, or we can acknowledge the simple fact that things change. Our relationships to things will also change. And those things will eventually bite the dust, unless we beat them to it.

## THE SIMPLE TRUTH OF DEATH

As far as impermanence goes, I think death is the form of change that scares us the most. I remember when I was eighteen years old, I had a very rough year. It began with the death of my grandmother. While I was still reeling from that death, several other people began to pass as well: my high school gym coach, a student at my school, my favorite client at my part-time job, my history teacher, my uncle, a friend's brother. One of the hardest deaths at that time was an eight-year-old child that I babysat. He was being driven home from a play-date when a trucker in another lane fell asleep at the wheel and drove right into the car. It was horrible. It was all horrible.

At the end of twelve months, eight people I knew and

many people I cherished had died. I felt like I carried a black mark, and that death followed me everywhere I went.

Looking back at it now, it was a bit like a Buddhist bar mitzvah. A bar mitzvah in the Jewish tradition is a ceremony that normally takes place when you are thirteen, and marks your transition from a boy to a man. Call me a late bloomer, but my transition from an innocent boy into a more serious individual came through this incredible year of loss.

Within that experience, I had a very simple choice. Our friend Sid had the same one. I could either hide from this intense exposure to suffering, or I could leap in and explore the simple truth of death. I leapt in. Particularly when considering the story of my eight-year-old friend, I came to realize that death can come at any time in our life. We can live to be one hundred, or we can get hit by a bus tomorrow.

Although it is a harsh reality to face, everyone we care about will die. A few months back, I was teaching a meditation class on this very topic. As part of the curriculum, there is an exercise where people are given the opportunity to sit in a chair in front of the class, and give their own obituary. One by one, members of the class would come up to the chair, sit down, take a breath, connect with their heart, and say, "My name is John Balanski. I was born on December 9th, 1976. I grew up in Queens, New York. I too will die."

The point was not to get morbid, but to be able to fearlessly proclaim the simple truth of our existence. If you are born, you will die. This will happen.

The energy in the room was incredibly potent. The most memorable moment was when a man in his late twenties got into the chair and very boldly said his piece. He seemed confident and relaxed. As we sat there together, silently acknowledging that reality, I heard his fiancée begin to quietly cry. It was fine and good for people to get up and proclaim their own death, but she was trying to begin a new life with this individual, and she was struck by the idea that lo and behold, he too would die. This reality was heartbreaking, but it opened her up to a new level of appreciation for her future husband.

## Contemplation on Death

I don't necessarily suggest getting up in front of a crowd of people and announcing that at some point you will die. Instead, you might want to work with a common contemplation: "Death comes without warning; this body will be a corpse." I recommend rolling that around in your head if you are looking to explore this important topic.

As with other contemplations, the general idea is to open by grounding yourself in shamatha, and then to take a set period of time to keep coming back to the phrase over and over again. In some sense, this is just like shamatha meditation when you continuously come back to the breath, only now we come back to this potent sentence.

In the course of your practice session, try to tease out how this phrase may apply to you. Notice what emotions come up. Does it scare you to think that you will die? That you won't know how or when it might happen? If death came tomorrow, would you feel sad for not being able to accomplish everything you wanted to do? Would you be able to accept it?

After five minutes of continuously coming back to that phrase, you can drop the words altogether, and just rest with whatever emotions have come up. Just stay present with that feeling. Lean into it, like the fearless garuda. After a few minutes, you can return to shamatha.

It is said that a good contemplation practice leaves you with a very powerful aftertaste. A high-quality contemplative session often feels very real and immediate. You are bringing intellectual concepts down to earth and transforming them into personal experience.

## Leaning Into Death

It is one thing to conceptually think about what your body might look like when you're dead, or fantasize about what a nice funeral people would throw in your honor. It is another to be walking to a friend's house, daydreaming about your new girlfriend, and as you cross the street you suddenly hear a car speeding out of control, then screech to a halt just two feet away from you. At that moment, the reality that death can come without warning is an undeniable experience. If we can bring that sense of immediacy and reality into our contemplation practice, then we are doing a very good job.

To reiterate, we cannot just intellectualize the reality of death, or we will not be prepared for it. A few years ago I was out for a run in Boston. I had gotten lost, and was running across a street during a red light. A small bus was coming down the road; the driver was late to pick up some schoolchildren and was speeding so he could turn right at that light. We collided.

The bus was fine, not surprisingly, and I somehow picked myself up off the road and walked away with only a twisted ankle. If I had fallen even a few inches in a different direction, though, my head would have hit pavement and I might very well have died.

A few days later I was in Germany, hobbling around a Shambhala Buddhist conference. I told this story to the president of the Shambhala organization, Richard Reoch, who asked me what was on my mind when I got hit. I thought back, and clearly recalled thinking, "Well. This is interesting." I told Richard, and he said, "As far as final thoughts go, if that's what you're working with, it's not bad!"

Although I was feeling rather beat-up at the time, I felt pretty good about Richard's statement. I credited my calm thoughts at that moment of the accident to the time I had spent on and off the cushion leaning into my personal fear of death, trying to cultivate a positive attitude toward it.

While it seems morbid, it's important to take time to truly contemplate death, translating your intellectual understanding that it will occur to this experiential knowledge of its role in your life. It's like when you have to take a big test at school. You know it is coming. You can just occupy yourself with distraction and fun, but when the time comes to take the test, you will be unprepared. Instead, if you turn your mind a little bit to the material at hand, you can enter into the situation feeling prepared and calm. That is how the garuda faces death.

Fundamentally, we are exploring the relationship between fear and the nature of reality. Through exploring reality, we can see fear for what it is: an emotional hook that will drag us down. The world is fluid and changing, so we will constantly be presented with these hooks of fear. No matter where we turn, we are faced with the irrefutable truths of impermanence and death. It is not the world that makes us live in fear of change and death—we do that to ourselves. We need to work with these experiences, leaning into them, in order to ride the energy of our lives.

We can try to hide behind a palace of our own making, applying makeup or hiding our elderly in an effort to ward off change and death. It won't work. No matter how high we build our towers of security, they too are subject to impermanence. We ourselves are subject to impermanence. Our loved ones are subject to impermanence. Hiding is an untenable solution.

It is said that the garuda shrieks a fearless proclamation of reality as he soars across the sky. In other words, he proclaims the truth. He acknowledges the scary aspects of his life, including aging, sickness, and death, and fearlessly engages them with an open heart. He is present with the reality of his situation. Instead of fighting these truths, he embraces them.

When we follow in the path of the garuda, we too can free ourselves from the exhausting effort to find lasting certainty and security for ourselves. We don't have to fight reality. It can be liberating to see our world clearly, just as it is. When we acknowledge our impermanence, as well as the impermanence of everything around us, we can find true appreciation for the way things are. By studying impermanence and death, we can see the sacred aspects of this very moment.

# 17 / REJOICING IN COCONUTS OF WAKEFULNESS

In the garden of gentle sanity, may you be bombarded by coconuts of wakefulness.

—*Chögyam Trungpa Rinpoche*

The garuda soars through his life, never touching the earth. There is grace and courage in his flight. He is the epitome of a being who is able to live without clinging to solid ground. In other words, he is comfortable with feeling groundless.

For most of us, this idea seems impossible. There is an inherent paradox in being comfortable with discomfort. It is no surprise that thus far you may have treated feeling groundless as a painful experience, something you want to avoid. Our entire society is based in avoiding the uncomfortable aspects of life. If we follow the garuda's lead and lean into them, we are taking an unconventional approach. Still, we have explored many set concepts in our journey so far, so it only makes sense to see if we can turn our contemplative mind to uncomfortable situations and see how we can face them fearlessly.

We can acknowledge that things change and that death is inevitable, but when it happens to us, and in a big way, we're often unprepared. It may feel like we are being bombarded, as Trungpa Rinpoche wrote in the poem at the beginning of this chapter. Today, you could be going through your daily routine, your own personal garden of gentle sanity as Trungpa Rinpoche might call it, and then all of a sudden a coconut hits you on the head. A coconut might take the form of a phone call from your father telling you that your mother has been rushed to the hospital. It could be waking up next to your girlfriend and being told that things aren't working out. It could be walking into the office on Monday and finding out that you are newly unemployed.

When a coconut hits us on the head we can curl up in pain, wondering why we have been singled out as the recipient of uncertainty and change. In fact, most of us have spent years honing that specific response. When we see a drastic change in our life, our first reaction is to shut down. Emotionally, we curl up in a ball and hope that change will go pick on someone else. This is quite foolish, because we know that impermanence is inherent in all of our lives.

As an alternative, we can begin training in the example of the garuda by flying headfirst into whatever uncomfortable situations arise. When we get hit by a coconut, our first step should be applying vipashyana to the situation, carefully analyzing where the coconut came from. When we begin to become inquisitive with our pain and groundlessness, we often learn a valuable lesson.

For instance, in the examples above, you might see that your mother's poor health is a direct result of years of neglecting her body. This knowledge may inspire you to take better care of your own. If you get dumped, you can listen to why your partner feels she has to end things so you can gain closure, and look to cultivate a different form of relationship in the future. If you get fired, you might have to sit through an earful about your poor performance, but maybe something—even if it's just one little thing—rings true, and you can learn from this truth and apply it to your next job.

By applying an inquisitive mind to your uncomfortable coconut situations, you are doing two things. The first is dropping your set notions of what is going on in the uncomfortable scenario. Thus far we have been talking about not getting hooked by strong emotions. The garuda goes beyond that practice, and does not even get hooked by set notions, which in some sense are the wellspring for strong emotions themselves. By training in not solidifying the way you think things ought to be, you are cutting through years of habitual response mechanisms, and beginning to see your discomfort in a more lucid manner.

The second thing you are doing by applying an inquisitive outlook is starting to open up to a wider awareness about the situation. You are wiping the passion, aggression, and ignorance out of your eyes. You have dropped the way "I" think things ought to be. In fact, you are dropping the "I" altogether.

Within that wider awareness, untainted by your "me"-tinged glasses, you can clearly perceive the ephemeral nature of your own discomfort. Like all things, the difficult situation, as well as the intense emotions around it, is impermanent. You can find true joy in that discovery. It is liberating to see that the coconut that hit you is not so solid after all. Like all things, it too will pass.

Having applied your inquisitive mind to discomfort, you have one more tool for working through it: your open heart, or bodhichitta. The path of the garuda is about leaning in when groundlessness arises, investigating it and seeing it for what it is, and the hardest part, which is embracing it. When difficult situations arise, we have to exercise our open heart further than we normally feel comfortable in order to accommodate them. We have to change our very view about discomfort in order to work through it. We have to cut through our habitual inclination to shut down and hide from fear, and instead dive right in, allowing our openness to transform it.

Discomfort and uncertainty are not new. They have been coming up for every creature since the dawn of time. One of the most common ideas about our universe's birth is the big bang theory. This is not a "Things started off going as planned and only got more comfortable with time" type of theory. It is the idea that a big explosion took place, and out of that explosion the universe burst into existence. From that time, you can say that big and small explosions have taken place constantly, especially on our particular world, ranging from Hiroshima to the time you bumped into someone on the street and they swore at you. The universe is in a constant state of chaos and change; whether we cringe from it or respond with an open heart is our choice.

Atisha knew this all too well. He clearly systematized and articulated an approach to bodhichitta known in Tibetan as *lojong. Lo* can be translated as "mind," specifically the mind that goes, and *jong* means "training." It is the mind that goes to be trained, or mind training. Atisha produced the fifty-nine lojong slogans as a way for us to turn our mind to cultivate bodhichitta, and to help us figure out how to respond to our explosive, mishap-ridden world.

One such slogan is "When the world is filled with evil, transform all mishaps into the path of *bodhi.*" Evil can be considered in numerous ways. There is the evil of tyranny and oppression, and the evil of spitting in someone's food. It's a very subjective term. For our purposes, we can consider this slogan as pointing to the fact that the world is full of confusion, as well as the discomfort that is a direct result of that confusion.

Taking discomfort as our premise, we are being encouraged by Atisha to consider any negative circumstances that come up as opportunities. Through entering into the path of bodhi, of openness, we can transform all mishaps that come into our life into golden opportunities to be fearless. Taking Atisha's view, we are turning our mind away from considering groundlessness as something to avoid. Instead, we welcome uncertainty because we can use each change in our life as an opportunity to open our heart further. We can look to the coconuts that bombard us as opportunities to wake up to reality. As a result of this shift in view, no matter what comes our way, we can treat each moment as a potential opportunity to cultivate humanity and tenderness.

The garuda is fearless and courageous, qualities that are

quite magnetizing to others. We too can live like the garuda, remaining curious about our life and opening our heart in a vast way, even when things get intense or scary. If we succeed in doing this, we too can be magnetizing. For one thing, everyone wants to be friends with someone who lives life to the fullest. This is what the garuda does in remaining truly openhearted with his world. He lives every moment in the present, making the most of his precious birth. Because he is always open to whatever arises, he is able to see his world clearly. Because he is not hiding from discomfort, he is open to possibility. He magnetizes good circumstances, as well as leans into the bad, because he is open. He is bodhi.

In Tibetan, the term *ziji* describes this particular type of courage. *Zi* means "shine," while *ji* means "splendor," or "dignity." In other words, the warrior who addresses their life in a fearless manner literally shines with dignity, and radiates splendor from their being. It is as if they cannot contain the radiance of their own heart. Everyone sees it.

Another more succinct way of translating *ziji* is "brilliant confidence." You can carry the confidence to relate directly with your life, instead of choosing to live and die in fear. You can be confident in expressing your heart, knowing that whatever wounds others might try to inflict on you are only temporary and impermanent. You can have faith that your bodhichitta can accommodate everything.

One way to clearly express confidence is by letting go. The whole path of the garuda is based on this concept. By following the path of the garuda, you are learning to let go of your solid sense of self and loosen your set expectations for the world. You are unhinging the trap of hope and fear, a trap that has held you down for most of your life. Part of unhinging yourself from that trap is leaving behind any deception you might hold about impermanence and death. Even when your life drastically shifts and you are left feeling groundless, you can take the opportunity to shake off that trap and let go into fathomless space. You let go into the realm of the garuda.

When you let go of the tight hold you have on your life, you are engaging two trainings. The first training is dropping expectation. You are cutting through years of habitual reactions, ways you have trained yourself to respond to pain, disappointment, and grief. You are actively unraveling the solid sense of "me" that has paralyzed you and prevented you from relating fully to your life.

The second training is learning to relax. We spend so much energy trying to constantly protect "me" that we have no idea what will happen if we just drop our shield altogether. What occurs naturally is relaxation. It is like adjusting a radio dial to find a channel: when we correctly tune in, the music comes through clearly. The same can be said for learning to let go of expectation: we naturally tune in to the way things are. Our world expresses itself beautifully, like a symphony of joy and courage that has been designed just for us. Within that space, we can finally chill out.

When you stop speeding about in your daily routine and just sit down on the meditation cushion, you are training in being present with the breath. You are learning to tune in to the way things are. If you then apply this principle of opening to your awareness to your everyday activities, you can see the world clearly. You utilize your inquisitive mind to discover the way things truly are. You open your heart to encompass the entire world, both the good and the bad.

Within this vast openness you do not cling to those labels, or any opinions or emotions that might be born from set expectations. Your problems are no longer problems; they are opportunities for wakefulness. Coconuts fall on us and we rejoice: Another opportunity to cultivate the big view of the garuda! Another opportunity to cultivate equanimity!

# 18 / TEARING APART THE PAPIER-MÂCHÉ YOU

So far during our discussion of the garuda, we have talked about all the aspects of life that he overcomes. In other words, we have examined all of the sticky areas of existence that make us uncomfortable: impermanence and groundlessness. When we follow in the garuda's trail and embrace those aspects of our life, we find them more workable. Since they are basic truths, we find that our energy is better used leaning into them rather than hiding from them. When we do so, we are able to break through to equanimity.

One dictionary I checked defines *equanimity* as "mental calmness, composure, and evenness of temper, especially in a difficult situation." We have been attempting to cultivate this level of composure in our calm-abiding, or shamatha, meditation. However, we cannot achieve equanimity without the second half of this definition: the difficult scenarios we are constantly presented with each day. These painful parts of our lives are actually opportunities to bring our even mindedness off the cushion and allow us to act like true bodhisattvas. A true bodhisattva leans into the hard times, and yet remains open and accommodating throughout their life.

In looking intently at impermanence and groundlessness, we are essentially looking at variations on a theme. That theme is how "I" protect myself from struggle, and simultaneously how "I" hide from my own open heart. This

"I" we all walk around with is often referred to in Buddhist terminology as our ego.

*Ego* is a three-letter word that can be used to imply that since the time we were born, each of us has constructed a set notion of who we are, how we respond to certain situations, and what we like, don't like, and couldn't care less about. We have solidified this ego through the years, ingraining both bad and good habits in order to make ourselves seem completely real and permanent.

From a Buddhist standpoint, this ego is a fallacy. In the same way that we cannot irrefutably prove that there is a god or gods manipulating our existence, we cannot prove that we are a solid, set self. We have examined how we age and change over time. However, until we start chipping away at this shell of an identity that we have constructed, we cannot hope to allow our bodhisattva activity to fully manifest and shine out to the world.

In some sense, the ego you create is a papier-mâché version of yourself. You have this body that you use as the core shell. From there, you layer on strips of personality, adding an interest in sports here, a favorite movie there, a funny facial tick on another side, and boom, you have created an ego doll. Consider the following set of contemplations an experiment in pulling those strips off the papier-mâché ego, and ideally tearing open that shell.

## CONTEMPLATION ON THE FIVE SKANDHAS

From a traditional Buddhist point of view, the self is seen as a conglomeration of five *skandhas,* or aggregates, that come together and allow us the illusion that we are a complete and solid being. The five skandhas are: our physical form, our layers of feelings, our perceptions, our mental formations, and the consciousness that holds the whole package together.

Take some time to engage this contemplation. While some

of the practices recommended thus far can be done sitting in bed in the morning or riding in a car, I suggest bookending this practice with at least ten minutes of shamatha before and afterward.

After sitting for a period of time, we will begin contemplating the first of the five aggregates, form.

## FORM

Start with a general contemplation, continuously coming back to the question, "What is this body?" Is it rooted in your head? Is the idea of your body based in your brain? Is it your heart? As you begin this exploration, look to see if your understanding of your body is based in its entirety. Is your notion of your physical form the image you see in the mirror each day?

If you believe that your body is a set thing, what would happen if you lost part of it? If you lost a finger in an accident, would you still be "you"? What about a whole arm? Would you still be "you" if you lost the ability to move?

Another way to explore set notions of your physical self is through selecting a particular aspect of your body and examining it fully. Take your hand, for instance. What is your hand? It looks pretty solid and real. However, since the time you got your first cut, you have known that there are layers of skin in your hand. Under the skin there is blood rushing through veins. There are muscles and bones to provide support.

Science has shown us that each element of our seemingly solid hand can be further broken down into cells. Each of those cells can be further broken down into molecules. From there we can consider that each molecule is made up of atoms. If our hand rests on our thigh while meditating, where does a hand atom end, and a pants atom begin?

Try these three contemplations for examining your form: examining where your body seems to be based, considering at what point your body would no longer be "you," and taking an aspect of your body and examining it to the point where boundaries around solidity become loose or fragile.

Conclude this part of the contemplation by turning your mind to the questions, "What in my form is the self? What in my form is truly solid?" After considering these questions for two minutes, return to shamatha briefly.

## FEELING

The next contemplation involves feeling, the second of the five skandhas. Most likely you have already been working with a strong feeling this week. Often when we get hooked by these feelings, it seems like we are nothing more than a walking embodiment of what we are experiencing. When we are newly in love, we walk through life as if floating on a cloud. When we are angry, there could be cartoon storm clouds circling our head; we wouldn't know because we're a ball of tension and aggression.

Whatever strong feelings have been coming up for you of late, take a moment now to lean into them. Begin by letting them boil up fully inside of you. Maintain your posture and hold your seat. Now contemplate the question, "Where does this emotion exist in my body?" Try to locate where in your body you are experiencing this feeling. Note the tendency to shy away from the emotion. Explore if the emotion is something you desire, feel aggression toward, or just want to push away.

After a few minutes of exploring the physical location of the feeling, consider other aspects of it. Does your feeling have a shape? Is it square? A circle? An octagon? What is the color of this feeling? Is it hot or cold? The more you begin to probe at the feeling, the less you will find to hold on to. Even if the feeling has led you around as if you were a dog on a leash, when you identify the feeling, you find that there is no one on the other end holding the leash. The leash itself does not exist. Your feeling, while seemingly real, has no actual substance.

After contemplating feeling, return to shamatha briefly once more.

## Perception

Proceed now to contemplate the third skandha, perception. As you transition away from using your breath as the object of meditation, turn your attention toward one of your sense perceptions. For instance, focus on what you hear. It could be traffic in the street outside your home, the sound of your computer humming on your desk, or the snuffling of your dog or cat. Keep coming back to what you hear, just as you keep returning to the breath in shamatha.

Now, contemplate the phrase, "Where does this sound exist?" Does it exist in the object or being that is creating it? What about in your ear? Where in your ear? What about in your brain? Try to identify the specific location for that sound.

You can then try this contemplation with your other senses, such as what you might see, smell, touch, or if you happen to have a tasty beverage in your meditation space, taste. Genuinely try to find a location within which these sense perceptions actually exist. When you are done with this aspect of the contemplation, return to shamatha again.

## Mental Formation

At this point, you can turn your mind to mental formations, the fourth aggregate that ties us down into considering ourselves as solid and independent entities.

As you engage your sitting practice, notice the different thoughts that come up. Instead of labeling them "thinking" and returning to the breath, use them as the object of contemplation. Whatever mental habits, fresh ideas, set opinions, or compulsions come up, feel free to get inquisitive with them. When a particularly juicy thought comes up, contemplate, "Where does this thought reside?" Play with this contemplation for a period of time, and when you are done, return once more to shamatha.

## CONSCIOUSNESS

The last skandha we have to contemplate is consciousness. Briefly touch on the previous contemplations once more. Consider this a retrospective on your previous meditative work: begin by engaging one of the methods of examining your physical form, then pinpoint a feeling and try to distinguish specific aspects of it, then take one sense perception and try to find its location, then move on to dissecting one of your thoughts.

From there, contemplate, "Where is this 'me' who is engaging this contemplation practice?" What or who is actually doing any of this meditation?

After some period of contemplation, relax your mind and drop all technique. Don't go back to shamatha just yet; instead rest in the space that may have arisen in your practice.

The resting period at the end of this contemplation is very important. As we develop insight into the way things truly are, we become more and more comfortable with letting go into space. We feel confident because we are seeing reality more clearly. That confidence inspires us to move deeper into contemplating reality. We begin to recognize that it is a mental delusion to cling to the idea of a set entity that is real and exists in a solid way, and as a result our belief in an ego and separate self begins to dissolve.

As we begin to relax into the reality that our ego is not as solid as we originally thought, we experience equanimity. Despite whatever difficult situations come up in your life, you don't have to take them too seriously. For instance, if someone tries to insult you, you can consider that this individual does not actually exist in as real a way as they might think. The insult itself is without any true substance, since it's a mental formation with no solid form. The insult cannot truly land because you yourself are not a solid landing ground for anything. It can be liberating to realize that there is no insulter, no insult, and no one to be insulted.

Your life is fluid and impermanent. Equanimity is the sense of being comfortable with that reality. When you see your world through the eyes of the garuda, you are no longer constricted by concepts of what you like, what you don't like, and what you feel neutral toward. Set opinions and prejudices seem like a joke because you know they are empty of any real existence. Fear is also not as solid as we think. From this discovery, we can come to understand that equanimity is beyond both hope and fear.

Just like the garuda, you can experience your world with equanimity. Examining your life in an inquisitive way can feel liberating. Through this work, you are cutting through that loosely constructed papier-mâché version of yourself. You are tearing away the strips of habitual reactions that you have cultivated over the years. Within that hardened shell resides space. Underneath all of our layers of concept is space. Within that space is bodhichitta. Having discovered our innate nature we can experience and touch our world directly, intimately, and free from concepts. This is the experience of fearlessness.

# 19 / BRINGING A SPACIOUS MIND TO SUBTLE ACTS

My mind is vast like the sky, and my actions are subtle like sesame seeds.

—*Padmasambhava*

The world is a constantly shifting, seemingly chaotic place. Throughout your life you are bombarded by reminders of change, aging, and death. Even the best-laid plans fall apart all the time. Furthermore, you yourself are not the solid, set entity you originally believed yourself to be.

Acknowledging all of this, you can drop your notions of how things should be and see how things truly are. You can follow in the trail of the garuda and relax your mind into an unwavering openness to the world, appreciating life in all its complexity. We do not have to sprout wings and a beak to act like the garuda; we can embody these aspects of the garuda when relating to our daily life: our 9 to 5, our home, our family, our money, our electronics, and going out.

## OUR 9 TO 5

At the end of an enjoyable weekend, most of us develop a sinking feeling in the pit of our stomachs. We don't want to go to work on Monday morning. However, the reason we are ruining the last hours of a perfectly nice Sunday night is not based on any current reality. It is not our existent reality at all. We might be watching a funny movie, and yet because our mind is already at work, we feel horrible. However, it is not work that is causing us such angst, it's our expectations of what work will be like.

Instead of buying into the popular notion that work is a drag, we can look forward to our job with a sense of joy, knowing that work is an opportunity to practice the path of the garuda, relaxing the set notions we have developed. We don't have to clock in with the punch card of "What I fear this day will be," but instead with a completely blank slate. In other words, we can consider our regular school day or workday as a chance to work with our particular habits of buying into hope and fear.

Instead of allowing yourself to get hooked by the trap of hope and fear, you can use your 9 to 5 to become inquisitive about those emotional states. Try to keep your mind open to whatever possibilities may arise. When you see yourself caught by the hook of fear, apply any of the contemplations in chapter 18 to dissect that strong emotion. If you leave a meeting feeling like things should have gone another way, examine that concept and see if there is any true basis to its existence. If you cannot find any, then let it go.

Letting go of your set notions of how things will or should be at work allows you to reconnect with a vast mind, and be spacious and open to whatever opportunities arise. If you have something in your 9 to 5 that you typically try to avoid, drop your expectations about what that event will be like. Lean into the seemingly difficult situation, and you might be surprised that you actually enjoy the experience; you might see new chances to progress both spiritually and at work.

## Our Home

When you are faced with a lot of difficult people, it is easy to see how working with them in a positive way can be part of your practice. However, when you're alone at home with time on your hands, you can still maintain a vast mind. You don't have to flop in front of the TV and space out. You can rest in space and uplift your home.

One way to consider applying the teachings on the garuda to your home life is by taking the advice offered at the beginning of this chapter by Padmasambhava: keep a big mind, but be precise with your actions. Some people like to think that if they dive into the deep philosophical aspects of Buddhism, such as the lack of a solid sense of self, then they have truly "got it." This conceptual understanding of reality is not that helpful. Often, these people end up being mean to their spouse, and their dishes are overflowing in the sink.

Just because the garuda is able to soar effortlessly and is never bound by conventional notions, does not mean that he does whatever he wants and ignores what is going on around him. Quite the opposite: he is fully in touch with his world. Instead of intellectually understanding the teachings of the garuda, try to train in maintaining vipashyana off the cushion, and you will see that an experiential understanding of reality will naturally dawn. In this way, you are utilizing these teachings to open up your mind to space, and you will still be able to deal with the day-to-day realities of relationships and home.

For example, think of what it was like when you last came home from a trip. It may only have been a long weekend, but you walked in and you immediately noticed something new about your kitchen. You saw a few glasses that you meant to put away but didn't. You saw that a layer of dirt had accumulated on the stove from lack of use.

Before you begin thinking about the way you expected your kitchen to look, take a few moments to see how your kitchen actually is. By observing closely, you can tell a lot about the mind-set you were in when you left. From there, you can start to clean up and bring your home to a standard you enjoy.

In this case you were able to physically remove yourself

from seeing your home and then observe it with a fresh perspective. In following the example of the garuda you could rest your mind at any point and engage this exact process. You simply walk into a room, drop your concepts at the door, and experience your apartment for what it is. Are you pleased with what you see? Are there things you want to change? Rest in vast mind, and then when you have analyzed the situation, go ahead and put on your yellow cleaning gloves.

Now, let's look at how to hang art like a garuda. Normally you might wander around and bash walls in with your hammer, hanging the art in different rooms and at varying heights, continuously feeling unsatisfied with the results. Instead, take a moment to relax your mind, free of any ideas about where the art should go. Survey your wall space just like the garuda surveys his landscape—free of concept. Move through you home, maintaining this mind that is as vast as the sky.

After a few minutes of resting in spacious mind, see what feelings emerge. If you are drawn to a certain area, explore it. If you feel that this is where you want your piece of art to go, now is the time to engage in actions that are as subtle as the smallest of seeds. Take a tape measure to the walls, determine exactly where the nail should go, and execute the project with great care and precision.

Out of the vast mind of the garuda, incredibly precise and subtle actions will manifest. This way of relating to the world can begin at home, but it is of course applicable to the rest of your life, too.

## OUR FAMILY

If we want opportunities to work with habitual mind, spending a week with the family is prime practice time. Not only do you have opportunities to lean into somewhat tense dynamics, but you get to see the reality of aging and impermanence in people you have known your entire life.

Often when we are on the meditation cushion, we are dealing with our own long-standing concepts of how we think things should be. In a family, concepts about what it means to be doing well career-wise, when it is an acceptable time to drink, or what age one should get married have lasted generations. In fact, a family ethos might seem impenetrable.

Still, if we are able to maintain equanimity even in the face of tense family dynamics, we are essentially undercutting these long-standing notions of how things should be. Just by remaining open in the midst of stress-ridden conversations, you are unraveling the ball of yarn that is your habitual family dynamic. As difficult as it may sound, by maintaining equanimity in the midst of tension you are helping everyone else calm down as well.

Even if you are the sort of person who has an especially lovely family dynamic, it can be painful to see the effects of time on those you love. Acknowledging the reality of your family situation and embracing it is the practice of a warrior embodying the garuda. To cut through your own layers of how you hope things will be in your family, and instead remain open to how things actually are, is a true practice of bodhichitta.

You can see both the good and the bad parts about your particular family dynamic, and within that feel tremendous love and tenderness for those individuals who have been with you your whole life. Instead of falling into set dynamics, you can undo family habits and maintain a spacious mind, free of giving in to set notions of how things ought to be.

## OUR MONEY

In the tiger section, we investigated our personal relationship to money, and in the section on the snow lion, we considered how to use money as a positive influence on the world. The path of the garuda is in realizing that money is not as solid as we may have originally thought, and as a result, our relationship to wealth is also malleable and fluid.

The warrior who follows the example of the garuda applies the teachings on change and the fluidity of reality to their relationship to money. For example, think back to the last time you took money out from an ATM. At the end of that process, it is likely that a number was printed on the receipt indicating how much money you have in your account. If the number seemed high, you felt hope, and if it seemed low, you felt fear. However, it is just a number. It does not have any lasting substance.

Looking at the money in your wallet, it too is somewhat ephemeral. It is just paper and metal. It is only worth the amount that we as a society imbue it with. It is a conceptual tool to help us prove that we have earned something through our labor, and also allow us to trade for goods and services. Money itself cannot hurt us; it is the concepts and emotions we attach to these numbers and pieces of paper and metal that cause us angst.

We do not have to layer our relationship with wealth with our millions of hopes and fears. Instead, we can realize the empty and fluid nature of money in its various forms. When we see money in this way, we are freeing ourselves from a fixed mind about what is and is not possible. Having loosened our conceptual relationship to wealth, we can begin to view money as a means for enriching ourselves. We see how pride or a poverty mentality might rear its ugly head, and instead of indulging those trains of thoughts we relax our mind more, allowing these thoughts the space to arise and dissolve without much effort on our part.

When we engage our relationship to money in this way, we are claiming the energetic quality of it in a way that becomes very powerful. We are not a slave to our concepts about what we are worth. We know money to be as fluid and changing as everything else in the world, and we see that we can use this building block of society for our own personal growth. Adopting this attitude of freedom from concepts, we can utilize money in a way that benefits ourselves and others. Turning our contemplative outlook to the most basic elements of our life, such as our relationship to money, allows us to expand our view on what we have to offer on all fronts.

## Our Electronics

At some point during my lifetime, society became dependent on small electronic devices. It used to be that if you got lost, you would have to look at a map, or talk to another person and hope that they were directionally savvy. Today, people just take out their phones, and quickly discover their exact location. Directions to wherever you want to go are just a click away.

There are not many things you can bank on in today's society, but electronics breaking down is surely one of them. Having examined the world around us, we know that everything is impermanent. It should not surprise us when the devices we depend on also falter and fall apart. Yet many of us do feel surprised and angry when the technology we have come to depend upon falls subject to the same forces of nature as everything else.

I find it fascinating that technology has simultaneously made it possible for us to be in better touch with one another, yet also has made our communication less clear. You may receive an e-mail from someone, but even after twenty readings, you still do not know if the person is joking around with you, or if they are actually angry and attempting to be hurtful.

Given the prevalence of technology in today's society, we cannot just simply ignore these electronic devices. All of us have something that we consider both helpful because it makes our life easier, and difficult because it sometimes leads to confusion and eventually ends up falling apart.

The path of the garuda is to engage the various devices that exist in our life, be it a laptop, cell phone, or television, without getting attached to hope and fear. We can own the latest tech toys and attempt to utilize them for good, but at the same time acknowledge their basic nature. Just like a new relationship or new job, a new gadget will not be able to bring us happiness. Knowing that true joy comes from being present with whatever arises, it is up to us to figure out how best to employ technology in a way that allows us to further that goal.

## GOING OUT

You can be a "good" Buddhist and still go out on a Saturday night. The important thing is to not check your meditative mind when you check your coat, but to maintain it wherever you go. By maintaining an open mind, you can see reality more clearly and know how to act in a good and decent manner.

If you go out with friends to a pub, notice how long you are able to remain free of concepts. You might immediately start checking people out. From there, you give in to the three basic reactions: "She's hot. I want her"; "She's dumb, get her away from me"; or "I can't tell if that's a ring on her finger so I'm going to ignore her."

As you approach the bar, see if you can relax and just be present with whoever you're out spending time with. Maintain some sense of openness to the evening and the company you keep, and just see what emerges. If you end up in a sticky situation at some point, you will be able to see how best to react if you were actually present as the situation unfolded.

When you keep an open mind instead of trying to zero in on having a perfect night, you often end up having a fun experience. Not because you manipulated it in any way, or planned it to be so, but because you relaxed and went with whatever opportunities came up. In fact, when you try to manufacture fun, your evening will never live up to your expectations. It is only through truly relaxing with what comes your way that you will be able to enjoy yourself.

A great example of this is New Year's Eve. Every year, people develop a set plan that they think will maximize their potential to have fun. It might include bringing a few friends to their place or jumping around from one party to another, but when the clock strikes midnight they expect to be having the time of their life. With this incredible amount of expectation, it is no surprise that most people feel let down on this night. Year after year, thousands of people try to conceptualize an enjoyable experience and make it into a reality, without realizing that if they relaxed their concepts about how New Year's Eve should be, it would probably be great fun.

This New Year's Eve, I suggest trying to remain open to whatever comes up. Drop any set plan or idea of what the night should be about. Even if you have an idea of how the evening might start, just enter the situation without thinking about where you will be at midnight. Enjoy the evening with old friends. Be open to meeting new friends if they come your way. Don't try to have a great time, just let yourself have a great time. You can check your notions of what should happen at the door and relax. If you enter into the evening without set goals, I am sure you will have a fantastic night.

Through engaging the path of the garuda, we are learning to hold a vast and spacious mind in all situations, be it at work, at home, with the ones we love, with our money, with our electronics, or going out for a wild night. We can do all of these things if we learn to balance an understanding of how the world around us works with the equanimity of the garuda.

When we relax into opening up our mind and heart fully, then our actions will naturally flow from that vantage point. We can follow Padmasambhava's words of advice, and maintain a vast mind while being open to performing subtle acts that benefit ourselves and others. We don't have to think through every scenario. We don't have to plan every minute of the day. We can go with the flow of our life, and relax into freedom.

## PART FOUR

# RELAXING INTO MAGIC

# 20 / SINGING A VAJRA SONG (IN THE SHOWER)

I've got the magic in me.

*—Rivers Cuomo*

Basic goodness is important. By studying the initial three dignities of the tiger, the snow lion, and the garuda, we are essentially just studying how to connect with our innate wisdom and how to use it as a moral compass. The various qualities we contemplate in connection with the dignities can aid us in connecting with the world and opening our heart to others. The generator for all of our awake activity has been, and continues to be, our basic goodness.

The common theme through each dignity is that we keep coming back to being present, in this very moment. If we want to be happy with our everyday life, we need to be in it. If we want to learn how to be of benefit to others, we need to be present in order to see how best to help. Our whole path of exploring these dignities keeps reinforcing the notion that we need to connect to what is going on right now, and when we are right now we are connecting with our own goodness.

There is one fundamental shift though, as we enter the path of the fourth dignity, the path of the dragon. We move away from training in how to be something altogether, and instead just relax and *be* in the world. In engaging the path of the dragon, we are truly being present with our lives through continuously manifesting our innate wisdom. We are learning to let our goodness flow effortlessly. Most important, we use everything around us as opportunities to express this innate beauty.

This is the realm of the Vajrayana teachings. The Vajrayana follows in the vein of the Mahayana tradition in that you are taking everyone else in the world as part of your path of compassion. You base yourself in the Hinayana discipline of taking good care of yourself, and you are still living the Mahayana ideal of having a life that benefits others. However, the Vajrayana is not just about how to play nicely with the people in your life. It is not just your annoying boss or noncommittal lover who qualify as part of your path. The Vajrayana is based in looking to everyone and taking every-*thing* as an opportunity to be awake.

Exploring the Vajrayana, your path is that SoCo and lime shot on a Friday night. Your path is that candy that you keep stashed in your desk meant only for you. Your path is that guilty pleasure song that you sing in the shower. Everything you do in your day is an opportunity to practice, whether anyone interacts with you or not. Even if it's just you singing into your bar of soap, completely alone in your apartment, this path is about continuing to manifest your basic goodness.

The Vajrayana path is based in looking at all the nitty-gritty parts of your life that you normally gloss over, and instead contemplating, "How can I express my innate wisdom here?" or "How can I express my basic enlightened qualities?" This means looking at the various aspects of your life that you might normally consider vices, and instead looking to them as opportunities to practice meditative mind.

The question about expressing your basic goodness may seem silly when singing that guilty pleasure song in the shower, but it's still worth doing. Think about the times when you are completely alone and you know that no one is going to judge you but you: Are you truly open and free? Or are you filled with self-loathing and doubt, whispering into the soap, trying to cover over your heart?

As we explore how in touch or out of touch we are in manifesting our innate goodness, we can apply the gentleness of the tiger, not judging ourselves harshly, but using each inquisitive act as an opportunity to celebrate how far we have come from when we first started practicing meditation. We continue to be kind with ourselves and maintain a nonjudgmental attitude even at the Vajrayana level. Especially at the Vajrayana level.

*Vajrayana* is a Sanskrit word that can be translated as "indestructible vehicle." *Indestructible vehicle* is not simply a cool moniker for a Buddhist lifestyle (although it is that as well). Rather, the term points to the one aspect about ourselves that we cannot reason away, gloss over entirely, or tear apart. The Vajrayana path is about understanding and then expressing the one thing that is truly indestructible: our own wakefulness.

One term that you may have heard in relationship to the Vajrayana is *tantra*. Sometimes this same vehicle is referred to as the Tantrayana. One way to define *tantra* is "continuity." When used in this way, the word refers to the continuity of wakefulness. The path of the Tantrayana is based in continuously remaining open and in touch with our basic goodness. It is saying that there is no time for a break in our practice; we need to always be in tune with our heart and act accordingly. If we are able to be awake with every aspect of our life, then we are walking on the path to enlightenment.

After meditating for a few months or years, you may feel that you are not awake in every aspect of your life. If so, you are not alone. In fact, most of us have a hard time being open, even when it's just us in the shower singing Spice Girls songs. This is because we have not developed deep trust in our basic goodness.

In some sense, the Shambhala Buddhist teachings are very simple. Throughout each of these four dignities, we keep returning to being open to our life. We keep touching on the generator of our compassionate activity, which is our open heart. We keep referring back to the source of our ability to be so open, which is the fact that we are basically good.

Still, even if we are devoted to living a kind and sane life, we don't necessarily walk around always trusting that we are, at our core, embodiments of basic goodness. Thus, if we want to emulate the dragon, we have to trust in our basic goodness. Being a pawo, one who is brave, is based in having the courage to overcome the nagging voice of society that has whispered in our ear since day one, telling us that we are not good enough, pretty enough, or smart enough. It means slowly dismantling our habitual tendency to doubt ourselves.

One way to think of this dignity is to equate where you are on the path with unraveling a ball of yarn. You have wound your sense of self so tightly that it's hard to imagine ever being able to be anything other than you, a big ball of yarn. That's just who you are; not string, or threads, but a ball of yarn.

Yet when you start to meditate, it's a bit like knocking over that ball of yarn. It rolls a bit, and a loose thread pokes out. That thread might be the strict routine you engage in every morning, or a certain "type" that is your ideal mate. In other words, it's a set concept. It's who you believe you are.

Through meditating, you start to see that things aren't as solid as you might have once imagined them; with a bit of prodding you can unravel some of your hardened traits. From that point of initial realization, you might be inspired to use different meditation and contemplative practices to tug at that ball of yarn. You gradually start to pull apart all the negative aspects of your life that you always wanted to do away with. At the same time, you don't look like you did before; that solid ball of yarn is more like a pile of loose string. This is like when you leave your meditation cushion and feel relaxed and spacious.

Right when you are feeling more spacious, with string everywhere, you start to hit some big knots. These knots have existed since you were a baby ball of yarn; they are your inherent doubts. They are your parents telling you that good children don't do certain things. They are the TV ads that say that successful people don't look like you do. They are your lack of faith in your own innate wisdom. They are what hold you back from just being spacious and open all the time.

Having pulled a bit at your negative traits and encountered the reality that you're not as solid as you may have originally thought, you still have a big part of your path ahead of you. You need to untie those knots. In other words, you need to directly address whatever uncertainty you have about your own basic goodness. This level of uncertainty is not simple day-to-day doubt. It is the underlying distrust that inspires a constant stream of thoughts that question your life and worth.

Once during a meditation program I was teaching in Boston, participants submitted questions anonymously, and then as a group we talked about how to apply these traditional teachings on the four dignities to those problems. One person submitted a note saying she was worried that her boyfriend didn't love her, because he didn't often say it aloud. During our discussion, we realized that in a situation like this, you can take care of yourself on one level by openly communicating with your boyfriend that you need to hear him express his love more often. That's fine.

However, the actual doubt that often exists within the layers of the "Does he love me?" string is a big knot: the uncertainty that you are, in fact, worthy of being loved. At different times I think we have all stumbled across this knot, or at the very least, a knot that looks similar to it.

We all have our own knots, and when we realize what that aspect of uncertainty is, we need to unravel these knots by looking closely at them and seeing them for what they truly are. If we don't stop to unravel our knots of doubt, this trap of uncertainty will manifest in a thousand different ways. We must dig in and address them with the clear-seeing wisdom of the dragon.

The dragon is not knotted up by uncertainty, but is fluid and playful in the midst of all the elements of the world. Be it a movie night or bar fight, the dragon is unconditionally there. This is because the dragon has freed herself from the trap of uncertainty. She has put her practice into action, and she truly embodies the wisdom of being fully present. Because she is not trying to manifest the Buddhist teachings but just acts in accordance with her heart, there is no room for her to be held up by knots of doubt.

There is a trick to following the dragon's example. We cannot reason away our knots of doubt and uncertainty. We cannot theorize a way to get rid of them. We can only relax our mind into our own innate wisdom. From there, our confidence in basic goodness grows, and the doubts naturally unravel.

As one of my teachers, Khenpo Tsultrim Gyamtso Rinpoche, once said, "Sometimes you need to put a lot of effort into practice and sometimes you need to take it easy, so both are important. Beginners need to put in effort, in the middle you relax a bit, and at the end you are perfectly relaxed. But again, if you are too attached to relaxation, then you become tight. So do not be attached to relaxation, either." Each of us must find the right balance of relaxation and effort to overcome uncertainty and reveal our basic goodness.

As we continue to grow more confident in our basic goodness, we shed layers of uncertainty like a lizard shedding its skin. All the times you were picked last for dodgeball fall away. All the times you felt inadequate at work slide off you. All the times you were rejected romantically get kicked to the floor. Through freeing yourself from uncertainty and being present enough to touch your own heart, you are shedding your dark and grimy skin. Underneath, you are ziji: confidence. You are bodhi: open. Underneath the layers of uncertainty, you are majestic like the dragon. You trust yourself, and you trust the world.

However, being majestic like the dragon does not mean that bad things won't come along and try to snap you out of that state of trust. This is not a set of teachings on how to be picked first for dodgeball. There will be pain, heartbreak, and sorrow. Pain is inevitable, but allowing it to cut you off from your own wisdom is optional. The path of the dragon is being open to all the experiences that life has to offer, and most importantly, looking to obstacles as further fuel for your spiritual path.

The dragon embodies the teachings she has received. As such, following in the path of the dragon is not about trying to transform you into something new. It is about waking up to who you already are. You don't have to work to be compassionate; you are compassionate. You don't have to train to be wise; you are wise. When you bring the two aspects of compassion and wisdom together, you automatically know how to act in the world.

The snow lion and garuda are paths of exploring compassion. The dragon is about resting in our wisdom. Together these dignities form a bridge between the Mahayana and Vajrayana teachings. In some sense, they are two sides of the same coin. The union of compassion and wisdom gives birth to skillful means. When you embody these dignities, you are maintaining a vast mind and acting in accord with your heart. The most skillful way to live your life naturally flows from that point of view.

The path of the dragon is looking to everything, the good and the bad, and reaching for it as if it were the most desirable thing in your life. We long to deal with our world directly, because then we can join compassion and wisdom to accomplish things. We can live our life skillfully. We are not burdened by uncertainty, so we are open and energetic in relating fully to whatever comes up. There is no choosing which things we like, which we don't, and which we want to ignore. They are all fuel for the fire that is the experience of now. They are all part of the glorious Vajrayana song we sing to ourselves, even if it is just us singing alone in the shower.

# 21 / THE AUTHENTICITY OF THE DRAGON

In the West, dragons have been given a bad rap. They are often depicted as the big scaly enemy who is holding a damsel in distress hostage. They shoot fire and eat people. The climax of many children's bedtime stories is when someone brave slays the dragon, and is then free to live happily ever after with whatever princess he saved.

In contrast, in the East dragons are often revered for their wisdom. They are benevolent creatures who help humans and represent some of the more primal forces of nature. They care for whoever needs their care. Both traditions meet at one point, though, which lies in the legendary creature's very name.

In the Western tradition, the word *dragon* finds its roots in the Greek *drákōn,* which can be translated as a "serpent of huge size." Both the Eastern and Western traditions depict the dragon as a large serpentine beast, replete with scales, talon-laced feet, and fire-breathing capabilities. The dragon is able to fly through the air, swim through water, and make a home on land. In essence, the dragon takes part in all the elements.

This Greek word for dragon is much more intriguing than a physical description, though. Many linguists have speculated that the word *drákōn* might have its roots in the verb *drakeîn*: "to see clearly." In the section on the garuda, we talked about leaving the ground and entering into space.

With the dragon we are learning to play in that space. We are learning to clearly see our world for its sacred and magical qualities, and delight in our experiences.

In Shambhala Buddhism, a phrase that is often associated with the dragon is that she is the "water of water, the fire of fire." The dragon sees the world clearly because she is not tethered by her own concerns or ways of protecting a solidified sense of "me." She interacts with the world with true freedom, and does whatever the environment calls for her to do. Living her life is not a struggle, but a rich and potent chance to create positive change in the world. If a situation arises in which the element of water is needed, the dragon will fly into the clouds and create rain. If fire is needed, she will breathe fire. She can see clearly what a situation calls for, and react in kind.

Utilizing the elements in accordance with situations does not have to be the stuff of legend. We too can see situations clearly and act accordingly, just like the dragon. When we are in a meeting and our coworkers drift off into far-off hypothetical scenarios, the way to embody the dragon is to bring them back to earth, grounding them in the reality of the issue you are addressing.

If your lover is lost in worrying about something, perhaps the kindest thing you can do is take him for a walk. There he can stop looking down at his navel and instead experience the sense of space and sky around him. He will have a chance to raise his gaze and breathe in fresh air, which ideally will snap him out of his funk.

If you arrive at your friends' home and you can immediately tell that your friends have been fighting, you don't have to sit down and try to hash out their differences. One way to embody the dragon is to see the cold atmosphere that has been created, and instead provide warmth. You don't need to breathe fire out of your mouth at that point, but you can provide nourishment and warmth by fixing your friends tea or making a lighthearted joke.

You yourself might feel on fire at times. Perhaps you went

on a hot date and felt a burning passion, but now you are alone in your apartment. The path of the dragon is quite simple in this case: take a cold shower. Throughout your day you constantly meet with opportunities to engage the elements in simple ways that can create space and delight in those around you.

## THE FOUR KARMAS

The fact that we have not seen a dragon in person does not mean we have to make the path of the dragon too metaphorical. The dragon is incredibly practical, because she sees situations clearly. She has developed a mature sense of prajna. She knows that in some cases she will need to be diplomatic and pacify issues that arise. In other cases, she will have to add her insight or opinion to enrich a conversation. Or she might decide to magnetize new factors to solve a problem. If absolutely necessary, she may even need to be harsh and act in a destructive way, but with the intention of benefiting others.

These four ways of relating to situations—pacifying, enriching, magnetizing, and destroying—are known as the *four karmas*. This is not karma as in "what goes around comes around," or in the larger sense of meritorious and nonvirtuous actions that affect future lives. The simplest translation of the word *karma* is "action." These are four types of action that we can engage in, which will each produce different results. Some may win us more friends than others, so it is important to cultivate the aspect of the dragon that knows how to read a situation correctly.

When faced with an obstacle, the dragon might react in accordance with what needs to happen by utilizing one of the four karmas. The dragon is not layering on how "I" think things ought to be, and as a result, the dragon can see what other people need to have happen. Sometimes that level of compassionate activity feels positive, like when she praises someone for their good work. Other times it might feel more negative but is still compassionate, such as when she tells her friend to leave an abusive spouse.

Just like the dragon, when you are able to stop only thinking about yourself and your point of view, things start to click a bit more. You see what needs to occur, even though other people may not have yet reached that same conclusion.

Think back to the last time someone told you some shocking news. How did you react? Did you start giving advice immediately? Did you come up with different ways that you thought the situation should have been handled? Take a moment and just reflect on how you handled that news.

Now think about what it would have been like if you had heard the news and then just rested your mind, relaxing with the news and letting it soak in. Perhaps if you had taken a bit of a gap before reacting, you might have come up with exploratory questions before jumping to a conclusion. You might have sat back and let the situation unfold until it was obvious you should react or get involved in some way. Instead of trying to manipulate the situation in any way, you could have rested with it, waiting until it was appropriate to act. Sounds a bit nicer than what you might normally do, doesn't it?

The dragon rests in nonconceptual space until reaction is required. She knows that in many cases, the wisest thing to do is not do anything at all. She is willing to give the precious gift of time to all situations, allowing them to work out on their own, and only acting when action is truly needed. As such, she is perceived as inscrutable.

## THE INSCRUTABLE DRAGON

Sometimes when I am spending time with Sakyong Mipham Rinpoche, I experience him as an inscrutable dragon. Sometimes people chat about very petty things with him, such as who is dating whom, or how certain people acted in ways they perceive as anti-Buddhist. I notice that both with my petty concerns and when people try to complain in front of him, he won't really confirm or deny what is going on. He won't, for example, weigh in and say, "Maron is too good for that Justin fellow" or "Why are you complaining about that person in the sangha when you're a jerk, too?" He has the unique ability to act as a mirror to others by not reacting in a perceivable way. He just remains spacious.

Within that space, people's petty emotions naturally dissolve. When that happens often enough, people are able to see how silly they are acting. His presence in these situations is hard to describe or categorize; it is inscrutable.

*Inscrutable* is Chögyam Trungpa Rinpoche's translation of the Tibetan term *spyang grung*. In essence, he combined two words, the former meaning "clever," and the latter meaning "wise." This clever wisdom is not about just knowing a lot of facts. It is the idea that you can embody wisdom, and from that vantage point, be clever about how to utilize that wisdom.

There is a playful quality to inscrutability. Sometimes when I ask Sakyong Mipham Rinpoche a question and he does not answer me in a direct way or he brings up an entirely different topic, I wonder, "Is he just messing around with me?" There's a chance he is acting as a mirror, allowing me to find my own wisdom by being elusive in his answer. Or there's a chance he's just being playful. More often than not, I believe he is acting both ways at once.

There is something confident yet relaxed about the warrior who embodies the qualities of the dragon. Watching someone who embodies the inscrutable dragon is like watching an extremely well-trained dancer. The dancer has tremendous strength. She has trained in all the moves she should execute, and can dance flawlessly upon request. However, her power comes from the fact that within the dance, she lets go of trying to get all the steps right and instead just dances. There is a confident and spontaneous element to her dance. Similarly, when we embody the qualities of the dragon, we are letting go of trying to be a good Buddhist and are just being truly human.

# The Qualities of the Dragon

## Sense of Humor and Delight

Where you and I might see big issues like war or corrupt governments as seemingly insurmountable and feel discouraged, the dragon maintains a healthy sense of delight. She knows that everything is impermanent, and that all problems are more fluid than we originally perceive. As a result she engages these large topics with a sense of humor. This is not just summoning up a joke to put others' minds at ease, but is based in the ability to feel joy even in the midst of dark situations.

Even with day-to-day obstacles, such as having too much work or missing the movie you want to see, the dragon finds delight. She maintains a healthy sense of openness, and is game for the possibility that even frustrating situations might present a chance for virtue and happiness. This is more than just grinning and bearing it in miserable situations because you want to be a good Buddhist. There is no such thing anyway, since "good" is subjective. The dragon is beyond the ideas of being good or bad, and she knows that what does not kill her will make her stronger. She rushes into adversity with a smile on her face, because she knows that only through such experiences will she be able to practice being strong and relaxed simultaneously.

We too can engage our life with delight, relaxing with the knowledge that even tough situations are impermanent. Sometimes when we are really taxed by the pains of the world, a sense of humor is exactly what is needed. We feel invigorated by the fluidity of the world around us, and that knowledge allows us to weather the storm and maintain a dignified attitude.

## Genuine Presence

The dragon is always genuine. Even if she is going to employ the four karmas, she will still be genuine. She will not lie in any way. If you are weeping over being dumped, the dragon will console you, but she won't tell you the little untruths you want to hear about your ex. If you're acting like a fool and causing confusion for yourself and others, she will call you on your garbage in a very straightforward way.

As frustrating as this might sound at times, the dragon is committed to being genuine in the most compassionate manner. It is pretty rare to meet someone who is truly genuine with us. When you first are introduced to someone, most people do not meet your gaze or will only talk about mundane topics. "What do you do for a living?" they might say. Or "How do you know our mutual acquaintance?" From there you can chat about whatever you normally like to chat about, and if you get stuck, you can talk about funny videos you have seen on the Internet.

Once in a blue moon, though, you meet someone, and without being particularly melodramatic, they will tell you what's on their mind. They will engage you with real information about who they are, and spend time asking you questions to try to find out what it is that makes you tick. This sort of person is more interested in getting to know you than trying to convince you to like them.

The dragon is that person at the party. She doesn't need you to like her, but you do anyway because she is genuine. Because the dragon is not worried about how she is perceived, she is free to interact with others in a way unencumbered by uncertainty. She manifests basic goodness, and people are magnetized by her genuine presence.

In the same way, we too can exhibit an authentic presence. When we do, we can live our lives in a very straightforward manner. We don't have to tell white lies, or sway others to our point of view. Instead we can manifest who we are, which is a gift to ourselves as well as to anyone we encounter.

### Magnetizing the World

In addition to attracting people to her like a magnet, the dragon also seems to attract all the sacred aspects of the world. In Eastern culture, dragons are said to possess some form of magic that binds them to the elements. Whether we believe in magic or not, we can experiment with allowing ourselves to rest in the gaps of our life and experience space. Within that space, we can begin to interact with the world around us and perceive it as sacred.

If you live your life with the same trust in your innate wisdom that the dragon does, you will find that things naturally go your way. It seems almost antithetical to the way we were raised. We have long thought that if we guarded our heart and only thought about how to protect ourselves, then we would be successful in life. Yet that methodology has only brought about sadness and frustration.

Instead, we can continuously be open to the possibilities that life presents us. When we are open to possibility, life naturally gives us what we need. When our heart is truly open, to the point where we see the suffering of the world around us, we can encompass everything we have been taught. We are able to express our sanity and our compassion. We are able to play in the little awkward or uncomfortable aspects of our life.

If we develop faith in the fact that we are basically good, then the next step is seeing this goodness in others. From there we can see that the whole world is basically sacred. Everyone around us has basic goodness. Even when our neighbors or coworkers stray from that root goodness and act out of confusion, the world around us still is good and magnificent.

The dragon trusts not only herself and her own goodness, but the sacredness of the world around her. She has faith that the world will provide her with what she needs in order to grow spiritually. When she is truly tapped into her world, she can see the most basic things as sacred: a mother and daughter walking to school together, with the mother walking slouched a little so she can hold her daughter's extended hand. She sees a spider methodically spinning his web in a quiet corner of the restaurant. She perceives a couple leaning against each other for support on the long train ride home.

If you want to be truly happy, you can follow in the path of the dragon. You can trust in your innate wisdom and allow it to guide you in skillful ways. This wisdom is what allows the dragon to clearly see her world. From that vantage point, she is able to relax with whatever comes her way. She is able to see magic in even the most ordinary situations.

We can live like the dragon. We can touch our open heart and express a sense of delight and humor, rather than getting bogged down by life's troubles. We can be genuine with whomever we meet or whatever we do. We don't have to hide who we are. When we accomplish this level of openness, we experience our world as sacred.

# 22 / DOING THE MILAREPA

Someone who knows that everything is mind
is able to use whatever appears as a resource

*—Milarepa*

There is an old Buddhist joke: The Dalai Lama approaches a hot dog vendor. The hot dog vendor asks, "What'll it be?"

The Dalai Lama replies, "Make me one with everything."

One spin on this joke is that the Dalai Lama buys a hot dog and hands the man a ten-dollar bill. After a few moments, the Dalai Lama impatiently asks, "Where's my change?"

The hot dog vendor replies, "Buddy, change comes from within."

At this point in your path, you may long for change, both internal and external. Maybe you want to be calmer, more focused, and more present in your life. At the same time, the world around us is in chaos and you likely long to help. While you may have seen some change already occur on the internal level, the idea of effecting large-scale change in the world as a whole can seem impossible at times if all you are doing is meditating and living your life as best you can.

My Internet homepage is CNN.com. I opened it today and saw stories on a foreign government being overthrown, rampant animal cruelty, the murder of a young child, and a headline that simply read: MISSING WOMAN KICKED,

SCREAMED. When faced with this much overwhelming misery, you might feel impotent. At those times, the question becomes, "What can you do for a world mired in suffering?"

In my mind, you have two options for how to live your life. You can give in to the uncertainty that surrounds us in the world. You can let suffering permeate your every fiber until you are like the *Saturday Night Live* character, Debbie Downer, constantly turning any news that comes your way into fodder for discussing how the world sucks. This path is based in letting the uncertainty of the world infiltrate our very being, so that at the end of the day we are uncertain of our goodness, yet very certain that everyone else is basically bad.

The other option is to have conviction in your own basic goodness and in the goodness of others. You can chose not to believe that everyone is basically bad.

However, if we choose this second option, we have to be practical. We have to realize that the world is not going to just get better at some point. It's not like we can elect a new president, come up with a new religion, or invent new currency, and all of a sudden the world's problems will be dispelled. It takes people like you and me, working to make ourselves kinder and more loving, to produce positive change in the world. We could have progressive leaders in every country, a wonderful religion everyone believes in, and enough food, housing, and jobs worldwide, but if people are only looking out for themselves we will still be in trouble.

When faced with the ills of the world, we can close down and become harsh. We can criticize others and shake our head at the news. Alternatively, we can develop a sense of delight in the midst of these incredible obstacles. If the hot dog vendor is right and change comes from within, then it must be based in that level of gentle humor that opens this chapter.

The dragon knows the world is constantly in flux, so when an obstacle presents itself she can laugh at its absurdity. "You, rampant unemployment, *you* think you can quell the human spirit?" she laughs. She knows that obstacles are only as serious as the mind makes them out to be. She has faith that people are inherently wise, and delights in that knowledge instead of becoming despondent because people are often confused and unable to express their wisdom.

If you look to the Kagyu tradition of Tibetan Buddhism, you will find a long lineage of meditation masters. These individuals were like you and me: at one point in their life they were mired in confusion, and at times they caused harm to others. Somewhere along the way, though, they encountered these Vajrayana teachings and transformed their misdeeds into fuel for a life of positivity and change. They learned how to look at the misery that faced their world, and approach it with delight and humor.

Milarepa is one of these individuals who contributed to the chaos and destruction in the world, but today he is considered one of the greatest saints in Tibet. Born at the beginning of the eleventh century, he spent much of his early life overwhelmed by the suffering that permeated his youth, and as a result he actually ruined many people's lives before he found the Buddhist teachings.

Milarepa's troubles began when, at an early age, his father died. Milarepa's uncle and aunt were greedy individuals who broke away from the deathbed wishes of Milarepa's father, and hoarded all of the family's wealth. Mila's mother decided that to avenge her family, Milarepa would learn black magic. He trained in the dark arts, and then he summoned a hailstorm and attacked his aunt and uncle during a large gathering, killing dozens of people. The local villagers got word that Milarepa was behind the attack and began to look for him. He responded with yet another hailstorm, destroying their crops and leaving the village hungry and destitute.

While hiding from the distraught villagers, Milarepa heard firsthand of the destruction he had wrought. He came to his senses and repented his evil deeds. When he heard about the great Buddhist teacher Marpa, Milarepa was overwhelmed yet again, but this time with happiness. He set out to meet this meditation master so he could follow a path that could teach him how to make amends.

Marpa did not just let Milarepa forget the sins of his past, though. He denied Milarepa teachings and told him he had to work off the price of the teachings through strenuous physical labor. Marpa told Milarepa to build a large stone tower. Milarepa toiled away for months, carrying large stones on his back. When the task was completed, Marpa pretended that something was wrong with the tower and made Milarepa tear down the whole structure. Then Marpa told Milarepa that he would have to rebuild it. This happened over and over again, with Marpa always asking Milarepa to rebuild the tower in a different manner or in a different location. Several years passed this way, with Milarepa, in essence, doing hard time for his grave misdeeds.

Finally, Marpa revealed that this process had cleansed Milarepa of his past sins, and that he was finally ready to pursue a spiritual path in earnest. You can imagine how ready Milarepa was to begin his practice, after he had spent so many years longing to engage in meditation. Milarepa studied with Marpa, and then he spent several more years meditating on his own in caves. Because of his sincere regret in causing harm, he renounced distractions and progressed along a spiritual path quite quickly.

Milarepa's meditative experience was a bit like one of those friction-driven toy cars: every time he built a tower, it was like pulling back on the car so the wheels are wound tight. When Marpa instructed him in meditation, it was like letting go of the car and watching it zoom off at top speed.

After meditating on his own for some time, Milarepa attained true awakening. He shirked the guilt and self-loathing he had accumulated and was able to manifest his innate wisdom. He returned to the old village where he grew up, the place where he was cheated out of his inheritance and caused havoc in return.

Without announcing himself in any big way, he began

to impart simple advice to those who stumbled across him on the outskirts of town. At one point, the aunt who had previously cheated his family approached him to ask forgiveness and received teachings so she too could become a better person. Over time, stories of his great teachings led many devoted followers to renounce their own confusion and practice meditation.

Milarepa lived until the age of eighty-four, and during his lifetime he taught many individuals the simple truth of how to live their lives in a sane and dignified manner. Many of his disciples, both men and women, attained states of realization themselves and went on to help other beings.

Even today, we can hear the story of Milarepa and see that despite causing great harm, he repented and became a spokesman for second chances. He inspired many people to renounce their own pain and doubt, and practice for the benefit of others. Despite his horrific background, Milarepa is often depicted with a slight smile playing across his face. He saw so many of life's greatest pains, but realized that so much of how he reacted to the suffering was all in his own mind. He could then use that knowledge to see the great pains of the world as a resource for his own meditation practice.

You can follow in the footsteps of Milarepa. Regardless of the various mistakes you may have made in your life or the pain you currently carry, you can smile. You can renounce the aspects of yourself that continue to weigh you down or make you miserable. Through applying the basic technique of meditation practice, you can turn your mind toward the reality of your situation, and view even the painful aspects as opportunities to remain openhearted.

This level of openness is the space in which the dragon plays. If you want to emulate the dragon, then you need to get serious about applying your meditation practice to your world. The dragon engages in the practice of tuning in to the simple beauty of everyday moments, even when there is pain in her heart.

You too can experience this taste of pleasure in the sacredness of the world while also knowing that pain exists within it. People are suffering throughout the world, but you can still rejoice in children playing on a playground right in front of your eyes. If you are able to connect to these simple delights, then you will be able to address larger issues, such as poverty and war, in a less jaded fashion.

There is a lot of confusion in the world. We cannot be love-and-lighty and think that staring at a kid on a playground is going to start a cultural revolution. However, if we do appreciate the simplicity and perfection of now, of this moment, then we are tapping into our basic goodness. From there we are able to share our heart more fully with those we encounter. Even if we just muster a few more Milarepa-like smiles, we are creating more openness and space in the world. Others may be infected with this new kindness bug and share it, until the ramifications are widespread and monumental.

Lately it seems like every new rapper will create a song about a dance move they invented. It could be teaching someone how to Dougie or how to do the dance from the classic 1989 movie *Weekend at Bernie's,* but there is something very catchy that people respond to with these songs, and they end up spreading like wildfire.

Sometimes when I'm out on a Saturday night, one of these songs will come on and everyone gets very excited. People who previously would never even look at one another have a five-minute window to do the same dance and smile at their fellow boogie mates. Even though I don't always like the message that comes with these songs, I feel the immediate sense of joy at the club when everyone can dance together.

This viral movement doesn't have to be limited to rappers. As meditation practitioners, we can create our own dance that meshes with these teachings. It is the dance of playing with the phenomenal world. Here is how to do the new dance craze, the Milarepa:

*Think of pain or confusion.* This can be pain you caused or that you experienced as a result of someone else's confusion. You don't have to turn to the most tear-jerking moment in your life, but acknowledge whatever suffering you feel that you are carrying with you right now.

*Do something nice for others.* You can live your own mini-version of building stone towers. You can simply pick up a piece of trash you see on the street, or let someone who appears to be in a hurry cut in front of you in line. Engage in some activity that allows you to move away from thinking about your own pain and confusion, and instead focus on the betterment of others.

*Rest your mind.* Just let yourself relax for a moment and appreciate the beauty of this very moment. Rest with whatever feelings of forgiveness for yourself and others that may arise.

*Smile.* This is the critical part of the dance—letting your basic goodness radiate out and touch others. See how long you can maintain this smile. Let the world see it.

When you are lost in your own world, or overwhelmed by the suffering around you, do the Milarepa. This simple set of moves allows you to stop focusing on your own pain and instead be of benefit to the world. You are turning your mind to the betterment of others, and through that you are able to touch your own goodness. Once you have reconnected to your wisdom, you can radiate that out and be of further good to the world around you.

I don't think it is naive to believe that if the majority of one nation's citizens did the Milarepa on a regular basis, true change would be effected throughout the entire world. The world is a fluid place; international predicaments may be long-standing or hard to solve, but they are just as much subject to impermanence as your latest gadget or your grandmother.

Because the world is so fluid, we can relax and try to make the most of our lives. This isn't a free pass to dance and drink your days away, but to consider every aspect of what you normally do as part of your path. If your path is touching your innate goodness and expressing it to others, you very well could be out dancing or drinking, but you will be doing those activities in a way that benefits the world around you.

We can study a great deal, both about worldly issues and about meditation, and accumulate a lot of knowledge. There is a common axiom, "Knowledge is power." However, true power rests in a very particular type of knowledge—the knowledge of how to help others. The root of true power is based in knowing how to exhibit compassion. Compassion can lead us to the wisdom of an open heart.

When you do the Milarepa and express genuine humor and delight in the world, it is refreshing for you and it inspires others. It is compassionate activity. You can share your natural sense of celebration with everyone you meet. They may then feel inspired to connect with their own heart and share their genuine radiance with the people they encounter. If you take every aspect of your life, both the painful and the pleasurable, as resources for offering humor and delight, then you follow in the trail of the dragon and make a true difference in this world.

# 23 / JOINING HEART AND MIND IN A GENUINE WAY

I recently saw a funny YouTube video. In the video, a honey badger is running around doing badger-like things. As is often seen on nature shows, the badger is hunting its prey, sleeping, and climbing around. Over the visual display there is an audio recording of someone commenting on the badger's activity.

The humor comes from Randall, the gentleman speaking alongside the badger's everyday routine, who continues to exclaim surprise at how bold and fearless the badger is. "The honey badger really just doesn't give a shit," Randall says. "The honey badger don't care!" He makes the honey badger out to be the epitome of self-confidence and talent.

While the honey badger may not have the same level of intelligence as the master warrior, he shares the same quality of just being who he is, without shame. We can all aspire to this level of carefree dignity. Even when the honey badger has a rat dangling from his mouth, he is comfortable with who he is. In the same way, the master warrior can engage in any activity, be it working at an underwhelming corporate job or going on a first date, with this level of confidence in their own basic nature.

## AUTHENTIC PRESENCE

The key to exhibiting this carefree dignity is expressing your basic goodness. When you are fully tapped into your own sense of worth and potential, you manifest what in the Shambhala world is known as "authentic presence." This is the phrase Chögyam Trungpa Rinpoche used to translate the traditional Tibetan term *wangthang. Wangthang* can be more directly translated as "field of power." It is the sense that when you are engaged in a life of virtue and kindness, you naturally manifest as a virtuous, kind being.

In today's society, if you are living your life in an authentic way, you may stick out like a sore thumb. Given the sheer number of people who are only looking out for their own interests, people will pick up on your energy if you are doing the polar opposite of that. They may not have seen you hold the door for that troop of older ladies going into the store, but that act leaves a slight mark of confidence and goodness on your being. This mark of confidence in your own goodness is stronger than any cologne or perfume you can pick up. It is *odeur de sagesse*, the scent of wisdom. It is inscrutable to the common eye, yet noticeable to anyone perceiving the world with an open mind.

The term *wangthang* is interesting. It signals that when you manifest your own goodness, you are literally exhibiting a field of power. As we discussed in the last chapter, true power comes from being willing to extend yourself beyond your own constraints and preferences, and being available to help the world around you. This field of power manifests when you are genuinely engaged in that level of virtue. It is indestructible power, the type of power that no one can take away from you.

In some sense, you can manifest this genuine presence by just being a good boy or girl. That is absolutely wonderful. You can help the homeless or adopt stray animals. This realm of virtuous activity is what the snow lion engages in, and it breeds bodhichitta, an open heart. We experience the delight of the snow lion when we exert ourselves on the behalf of others.

But there is a key difference between the snow lion's delight and that of the dragon. When we follow the path of the dragon, our activity is free from the dualistic notion of there being a "me" that is helping someone "else." The genuine presence that the dragon exhibits is due to the realization that both the self and the world around us are incredibly fluid, and they are not as stuck and fixed as we once believed.

The genuine presence of the dragon is rooted in the knowledge that she does not need to expect any results from her good deeds. She has let go of clinging to personal comfort and fixed mind, and she helps the world in whatever way is needed. She does so not because she wants to feel good about herself or hopes to advance spiritually, but because this is what is required when she clearly sees the world around her. She is solid in her presence, and has goodness to offer. At the same time she is relaxed and confident that she can accomplish anything she puts her mind to.

Developing a genuine presence is based in experiencing *jnana*, the wisdom that can see reality as it is. *Jnana* is a Sanskrit word, which indicates a pure awareness of the world that is unencumbered by concepts. It is seeing things clearly, as they are. When you are able to base your perception in jnana, you can naturally join your wisdom and your open heart, or your intellect and your intuition.

When you think about someone who is genuine, truly genuine, they are selfless. When you talk to them, they listen deeply, not thinking about how best to respond or how they might react if they were in your position. They are willing to share their heart and their mind with you, without necessarily painting a picture of what they would expect someone like you to do. They are able to join their mind and heart as one, and just be fully present.

## Exercise for Opening the Heart and Mind

As an exercise, we can explore our own relationship to our heart and mind, and then look at how best to bring them together. I recommend beginning this exercise by engaging in meditation practice, so that you can ground yourself in the solidity of the dragon by being present with the simple act of breathing.

After five minutes of shamatha meditation, do an abbreviated loving-kindness practice, as was described on pages 100–102 in the snow lion section. Return to those instructions if you need to review this practice. Begin by wishing yourself happiness before moving on to images and qualities for someone whom you love dearly. After calling forth those images, then move on to a friend or companion. Then wish happiness for someone whom you feel neutral toward—someone you are not particularly attracted to or repulsed by. After that, take the plunge and wish happiness for someone you find extremely difficult.

Having connected to those individuals, dissolve the boundaries between all five of you, just as you did in the past. Wish them all true happiness. Conclude by radiating this joy out, dropping all concepts of how you feel about any given individual and just letting the love flow. Take a full ten minutes for this loving-kindness practice.

When you are done with that practice, do not immediately return to shamatha. Raise your gaze to the level of the horizon. Keep your eyes open and your gaze loose and unfocused. Relax your mind and drop all meditation technique. You will continue to breathe naturally, even though you are not focused on that sensation. Just let your mind rest.

After a few minutes of relaxing your mind, return to shamatha practice, once again grounding yourself in that level of stability.

When you have concluded your meditation session, think about what that experience was like. What was it like to touch your heart and expose it in a vulnerable way? Be very inquisitive and explore how that felt to you: Was it a comfortable experience? Did you have any physical reaction to it?

Then turn your inquisitive nature to what it was like to

just relax your mind without any meditation technique. Was it overwhelming to be that loose with your practice? Did you feel comfortable keeping your eyes at that level?

During this process, avoid any sense of judgment and do not cling to any sense of achievement. Just notice how you reacted to working first with your heart, then with your mind. After a thorough examination of that experience, try to identify any points in your practice where you felt that your mind was informing your experience in sharing your heart, or the opposite, where you felt that your heart guided your mind to relax fully.

## STAYING GENUINE IN THE MIDST OF CHAOS

The more we explore how to open our heart and relax our mind, the more we can manifest a genuine presence throughout our day. Even if you find you do not have a lot of time in your schedule to practice, you can take advantage of little moments throughout your day to connect to a relaxed mind.

When you are waiting for someone at a restaurant or sitting patiently expecting a train, don't distract yourself by playing with your phone or by reading a book. Just raise your gaze and rest your mind. If you find yourself easily distracted, you can return your attention to your breathing, allowing it to anchor you to the present. However, take whatever glimpses of time you have here and there to connect to your relaxed mind and your open heart. At a certain point, this level of mind-heart synchronicity simply becomes a part of who we are.

If you are able to cultivate a genuine presence, you can shine even in the face of obstacles. My friend Jeff, for example, is a longtime meditator and a magician. While he is quite a talented performer, he is not yet at a point where he is raking in the dough. At times, Jeff has worked in crowded bars, burlesque shows, and other places where alcohol and sex are regular commodities.

Jeff once told me about his experience working at a club in downtown New York City. This bar has two worlds. One is a fun performance-based theater where drinks are expensive and the patrons are well dressed and good-looking. The other world exists behind the curtain where the performers are often doing hard drugs between sets or sleeping with the management to get ahead.

Jeff told me that it was difficult to work in such an environment; by and large his fellow performers were having a hard time staying healthy and sane. He only had a short stint working at that club, but throughout his time there, he seemed to be chipper as ever, and he made a large number of friends.

I have noticed this aspect of Jeff: wherever we go he connects very easily with people. He is not looking to make connections or get ahead by schmoozing, but he is genuinely interested in meeting people. He is comfortable with who he is, and people seem magnetized to that. Furthermore, as a meditation practitioner he has seen that virtuous activity brings delight to himself as well as others, and he continues to try to be helpful wherever he is. The end result of all of this is that Jeff exudes an authentic presence.

Jeff is able to work in these very intense environments because he is able to express his own goodness, even in the face of sadness and destruction. This is not to say that at times he himself does not occasionally feel sad, or that he doesn't make mistakes from time to time. However, he is able to constantly come back to faith in his own goodness, and he has been able to manifest that beacon of light in the midst of incredible darkness.

Jeff is not some enlightened master, but he is able to connect with this aspect of the path of the dragon—his authentic presence. Similarly, we don't need to reach some higher plain of spiritual awakening to contact our own wisdom and share that with others. We can be genuine now. We can be authentic now.

Often when people hear teachings on being genuine, they nod along and think it sounds good in theory. But then they wonder: once you are genuine, what's next? In other words, how does being genuine mean anything practical in today's mixed-up, crazy world?

Frankly, you should experiment with this idea and find out for yourself. I could tell you that being authentic makes a profound difference, but it's better if you apply these teachings and see if you notice a difference. Being genuine in this sense is not a path of just calling it like you see it, or not telling lies. It is about using your heart as a moral compass, and consistently coming back to the heart and letting it guide your activity.

When you are clearly attuned to what is going on in the world, perceiving it through the lens of jnana, then you will know how to act. You have trained in cultivating your intellect for most of your life, and you are now engaging in practices to further open your heart. You don't need anything else to be a genuine human being. Those tools alone are all you need to accomplish good in the world.

If you live a life guided by wisdom and compassion, you will naturally know how to address even tough situations in life. This is known in Buddhism as *upaya*. Translated from the Sanskrit, this can be "skillful or expedient means." It is the idea that if you are centered in your own authenticity, your mind and heart will guide you to skillful activity quite naturally.

The good news is that wherever you are on your path, you can connect your mind and your heart and be genuinely who you are, just like the honey badger. Furthermore, you can be confident in expressing who you are, despite whatever hard-hitting situations life throws at you. If like the dragon you are truly genuine, then you can share that magic with others. An authentic presence is quite rare in today's world, and as a result, it is more valuable than the rarest of jewels. This is what society needs, because a genuine friend is a friend indeed.

# 24 / MAKING THE ORDINARY MAGICAL

There's a power in every moment—a chance for happiness if you look for it. And it's every person's responsibility to find those moments and cherish them.

—*May Parker (the Amazing Spider-Man's aunt)*

When I was growing up, I read a lot of comic books. In many of them, something would happen to an everyday Joe like you or me and then—presto chango!—they would be blessed with wonderful abilities beyond their wildest imagination. Sometimes it would be superstrength or superspeed, or the ability to shoot laser beams from their eyes. Sometimes they would embrace their powers, and other times they would wish they had never received them. No matter how much of a curse the character may have felt their powers to be, I always envied them.

Over the years, I myself have had periods where I felt I had my own set of superpowers. After becoming a meditation practitioner and learning about basic goodness, I couldn't cling to walls or knock them down. Instead, I began to experience my own wisdom in new ways that felt superpowerful to me. I entered a process of discovering and experimenting with this wisdom, not unlike the costumed heroes I once admired did when they realized their newfound powers. I found that my innate wisdom was not supernatural in any way, but as I began to relax with my experience of this wisdom, it became supernatural to feel the power of everyday moments.

In terms of "abilities," I found that I was tuning in to my world in a hypervigilant way, being more open and caring with people, and more able to see the magic and beauty of the world around me. A key difference between me and the heroes of my youth was that nothing external happened to me. My innate wisdom was always there, but it was a magical aspect of myself that I had never paid much attention to. I always had the potential to experience my wisdom, but I had not turned my mind strongly toward cultivating that opportunity. Once I did, I felt more powerful and radiant: I was Basic Goodness Man.

We all can be Basic Goodness Man or Basic Goodness Woman. We all have the potential to unlock our heart and mind, and access these pure aspects of ourselves. Everyone in the world has the ability to slow down, connect to their heart, and be more accepting of whatever life brings them. You don't have to be bitten by a radioactive spider or exposed to gamma radiation to do that. You can simply be who you already are; you can be a fully genuine person.

The experience of your innate wisdom is not just a psychological condition in which you are able to live in a genuine manner. It is an experience of goodness in yourself and in the world around you. The dragon is considered an enchanted creature partly for this very reason. She has a unique ability to see the goodness of the world, and dance with the magic of her environment on a regular basis. She knows the truths expounded by the garuda: that life is precious and short and that we must make the most of it. She utilizes this knowledge as fodder to look for magic everywhere around her. As a result, she has an intimate, pure experience of the world.

We too can experience our life in this way. Think back to a time when you went somewhere truly beautiful. It could be a soft sandy beach where you gazed into a bright blue ocean, or a heavily wooded waterfall in the middle of no-where that you happened to discover. More specifically, try to think of a time when you relaxed and appreciated the experience of that dynamic force of nature. What did being in that space feel like?

I have always thought that there is something magical in places like that. Such places are primal, and untouched by our garbage, both conceptual and literal. When you experience a place like that, there is something mind stopping about it. You are overwhelmed by your perceptions, and this experience allows you to be truly open and authentic.

Because she is so solid yet relaxed, the dragon can see the beauty in any situation, not just these enchanting environments. Following in the path of the dragon is not solely about exhibiting an authentic presence. It is touching our own indestructible nature, our own beautiful wisdom, and then seeing it reflected in the world around us.

The dragon lives her life experiencing the entire world as sacred. She literally perceives the world through a view of sacred outlook. Even the sense perceptions themselves are considered extraordinary and magical. As Chögyam Trungpa Rinpoche has written, "In the Shambhala tradition, which is a secular tradition rather than a religious one, sense perceptions are regarded as sacred. They are regarded as basically good. . . . They are a source of wisdom." We can use our sense perceptions to experience the world in a full and deep way, just like the dragon. We can see the wisdom in the world around us.

When you are fully present with your life, little things often stand out that you would normally not see. The world as it is, when we experience it with our open heart and wise mind, is absolutely magnificent. I grew up in a rural area, and after a heavy snowfall, the environment would look pure and brilliant no matter where you turned. It was like the world had been blanketed in purity and pristine white.

Currently, I live in New York City. Before I moved here as an adult, a friend once described New York in the winter as a wet ashtray. Having spent the last few years here, I think that is a pretty apt description. Shortly after it snows, the walks are cleared and the snow is piled high by the busy roads. Then the snow is further defiled by exhaust fumes and dirt. It's hard to consider the world as sacred in this black and wet environment.

However, even if you are trudging through the snowy streets, your socks are soaked through, and you are late for work, you can find great beauty if you are open to it. You can just stop for a second, take a breath, and leave your sense perceptions open to whatever magic presents itself. It might be a catchy song playing in a cab driving by, or the image of a dog waiting for attention in an apartment window you are passing. When you look to the world in this open way, it will never disappoint you; there is always an opportunity for splendor to be experienced. This magic is very ordinary, and surrounds us all the time.

The next time you are on your way somewhere, be it work or meeting up with a friend, just take one moment and stop. Forget that you are rushing to anything, and just be present. Instead of turning your attention to your breath like you do on the meditation cushion, place it on the environment around you. Contemplate the question, "Where is the magic, the beauty, of this space?" Then relax your senses and see where your eyes are drawn.

More often than not, your eyes are not drawn to looking down at your feet, which is where you might normally stare when you are hurrying to get somewhere. Often, your gaze is drawn up. You might see a bird perched gently on a branch, or appreciate centuries-old architecture you never noticed before. Take just a moment to be grateful for the magic of your environment, just as you may have in the past when you were in a more secluded or natural setting.

I encourage you to do this exercise once a day for one week and see how your perception of the world changes. We rarely take the time to engage our world in this primal, pure way. This is an exercise in literally shifting you out of your habitual routine and cultivating a fresh take on how you experience your life. It is coming at your normal day with fresh eyes. It is employing the aspect of the dragon that is clear seeing. It is making the ordinary magical.

There are many stories of how Chögyam Trungpa Rinpoche cultivated fresh representations of this ordinary magic. One of my favorites involves the production of a medal that displays the four dignities of Shambhala.

As Trungpa Rinpoche traveled, people would make offerings to him in exchange for his teachings. Some of these offerings were small pieces of gold, such as single earrings or old rings that people no longer had use for or interest in. Many of us have this sort of miscellaneous jewelry, and we know that it is not very eye-catching. It might be a slightly scratched-up ring, or one-half of a pair of earrings that just sits in a drawer accumulating dust.

Trungpa Rinpoche cherished these pieces, and one day he decided to take this odd assortment of gold that he had been given and melt it down. It was reshaped into a medal, known as the Medal of the Four Dignities. It displayed the tiger, snow lion, garuda, and dragon in a beautiful way. He took other people's unloved and discarded relics, and transmuted them into something that was incredibly magnetizing to the eye. People who experienced the medal have said that it would stop their mind on the spot.

In the same way, we can take the rough elements of our life and mold them into something brilliant, magical, and mind-stoppingly gorgeous. This is not about turning lemons into lemonade. We are already lemonade; we are already basically good. Instead, it is about showing that we are genuinely lemonade: it is about manifesting sacredness. It is about our sacredness guiding our actions in a way that is decent and helpful to the world around us. It is about seeing the lemonade already present in our world, even when everyone else just sees a pile of lemons.

If you live your life with the same trust in your innate wisdom that the dragon does, you will experience the sacred elements of your life as she does, too. If you look to the world as a disgusting pit of slime, dirt, and nastiness, then you will experience your life as a struggle. Most people do, and perhaps you have in the past. However, if you instead look to the world as a sacred realm of possibility, you will live a life engaging in opportunity after opportunity for practice and joy.

As we discussed at the beginning of this book, our intention is important. If we intend to live a life based in trusting our own basic goodness, then we need to see the basic goodness in everyone around us. This needs to be a core view that we carry around with us: everyone is basically good. From that point of view, we can come to understand that the world around us is ordinary yet magical. If we hold the view of basic goodness as the center of our personal mandala, then we will live a rich and full life. Sure, pain and doubt may creep in at times, but our own open heart can accommodate them. Within that profound space these strong emotions are ineffectual, and ultimately they dissolve.

People around us are affected by this all-accommodating goodness that we display. Yet when we exhibit an authentic presence we are not just magnetizing good company; we are also magnetizing all sacred facets of our world. With confidence in our goodness at the heart of everything we do, the world naturally reveals its magical aspects to us.

The world does not need to be altered or changed in order for it to be sacred. It already is sacred. Similarly, everyone around us has basic goodness and is sacred as well. They may act confused at times, but they are basically good. We don't have to change anything about them, either.

There is, however, one thing we can and should change. What you can change is your point of view. If you want to live a life that is good and of benefit to others, you have to hold the view of confidence in your own goodness. You have to make that belief the central view that guides your life. From there you can learn to see the sacredness in others, and the magic in the world around you. You can start to tap into the beautiful aspects of your day in a potent way.

You don't need to do anything to experience your world in this way, other than allow yourself to experience your own wisdom.

It's a simple switch in view; you shift from doubt and uncertainty in your own wisdom and instead allow yourself to manifest brilliantly. You shift away from seeing the world as a problem and instead allow yourself to see its ordinary magic. In other words, you just have to be who you already are, and then like the dragon, you will live in a sacred world.

# 25 / RELAXING INTO YOUR LIFE

The problem is not enjoyment; the problem is attachment.

—*Tilopa*

As part of the Vajrayana path, we learn to take whatever comes our way and use it as fuel for our spiritual journey. At this point we are not theorizing about how to apply the teachings to our life; we see the necessity of leaning in and just doing it. As long as we are able to remain confident yet relaxed, we can enjoy the most basic elements of our world, viewing them as sacred.

As has been discussed in previous sections, it is not our family, our job, or our sex life that gets us into trouble. What gets us into trouble are the layers of concept and attachment that we place on all of these things. We are mired in thinking only about how we believe things ought to be. Our gaze is directed only at our own feet.

We should raise our gaze and turn our attention out to the world that surrounds us. From there whatever we see, hear, smell, taste, and touch can be considered as sacred. Whatever we encounter is not problematic, as long as we loosen our attachment to how things should be, and instead view our life as an opportunity to practice being genuine. With this in mind, let's explore how the qualities of the dragon inform our 9 to 5, our home, our money, going out, our mistakes, and compassionate leadership.

## Our 9 to 5

The warrior who embodies the qualities of the dragon is able to be strong and relaxed at the same time. When you are working with others, you can exemplify the solidity of earth as well as the large view of spacious mind. On a practical level, this may mean taking a three-step approach when engaging in a project with a group.

First, you can step away from the situation a bit. Don't jump to conclusions about how you think things ought to be accomplished. Just watch and listen at first, in a very genuine and patient way. It is always helpful to take some space and see what a particular project might call for. Furthermore, you then begin to see how others in the group are working on this project, and you can learn a great deal about how they believe things ought to go.

From there you can move on to the next step, taking an informed point of view. Having clearly seen the situation and genuinely listened to what others have to say about it, you can suggest what you believe is the best way to proceed. Ideally there is very little of "you" in your suggestion, and having given some space for a solution to arise, your plan is actually based in a complete understanding of the situation.

The third step is relaxing. In this process you have allowed enough space to arise so that you have manifested your basic goodness. You have also shown that you are trustworthy because you have genuinely considered others' points of view. When critiques come forth and alternative plans are put forward, your ego is not directly tied to your plan. As such, you can relax and go with the flow.

Furthermore, you can have a sense of humor and bring delight into what might seem like a chaotic situation. This level of relaxation is often a breath of fresh air in group dynamics. Your ability to take a stand on an issue but remain open to others' points of view will be experienced as a welcome change from society's norms. Even though you think you are just trying to solve a problem in school or work, you are actually changing the environment around you into one of authentic presence and deep listening.

## Our Home

The dragon is able to go anywhere and experience the magic of the land. However, her own home is a core area where magic can flourish. You can aim to establish harmony in your home by paying great attention to details: how your space is arranged, how often you clean it, where you hang certain things, and so on.

When you apply the precision of the tiger to your home, you are invoking a situation in which mindfulness and awareness can flourish. However, the dragon does not create such an environment because she wants to have a cozy nest to hide out in. She is committed to the welfare of others. This means that she uses her home as an opportunity to create an awake situation for herself but also for others. When friends and family visit, they feel perky and uplifted by spending time there.

We too can hold this motivation to utilize our home as an area that encourages an awakened mind-set. We can envision our home as an accommodating environment and an opportunity to make our world more available to anyone who enters it.

As Chögyam Trungpa Rinpoche has said, "When you express gentleness and precision in your environment, then real brilliance and power can descend onto that situation." You can follow in the path of the dragon and create a home that is an expression of brilliance and power. These qualities are not based in an egocentric atmosphere, but instead one that is created from the point of view of basic goodness.

An authentic person can create an authentic environment. Such an environment is inspirational to be in; it manifests dignity and is an aid to other people's states of mind. This is applicable not just to our home but our cubicle, our car, and other spaces that we frequently inhabit.

## Our Money

The dragon is bold yet loose about her relationship to money and wealth. She has the conviction that money, like all phenomena, is not as solid as one might actually believe it to be. As such, she is able to bring a sense of delight to her relationship to money. She relates to her financial transactions very deliberately, in a straightforward manner. She is not scared of how money will affect the world around her, because she has taken the time to contemplate how best it can be used.

You too can be brave and bring a sense of joy to your financial situation. Like the dragon, you can carefully analyze how you would like to wield money as the warrior's weapon, and utilize it in a way that is beneficial to yourself and others. You do not have to be too uptight about every transaction that occurs, but instead remain relaxed and confident that your spending habits are directly tied into skillful action, so long as you are truly in touch with your basic goodness.

If you have conviction in your own basic wisdom, you can let that guide you in how to make and spend money in a way that is beneficial. You can let your heart and mind be unified in expressing yourself through your relationship with money. You can witness all of your financial transactions as inherently magical, because they are aligned with your own goodness.

You are taking this aspect of your life that is so often riddled with confusion and pain, and instead presenting a genuine confidence in relating to it. This is brave, and it is worthy of feeling proud about. Doing so will inspire others to also consider how best to relate with their sense of money.

When you embody the dragon in this way, people are

magnetized to you. And inexplicably, because you are creating virtue in this aspect of your life, you may find that you are magnetizing wealth as well. New opportunities come your way, and you are open-minded and wise enough to embrace them. Relating to money in a direct and calm manner allows you to be of benefit and soak in the true wealth that is inherent to us all—our basic goodness.

## GOING OUT

The dragon maintains an awake mind even when out on the town. She needs to maintain her awareness so she can clearly see situations for what they are, and act accordingly. This is the key ingredient in her life.

For you and me, we need to experiment with how this might play out. Can you maintain mindfulness when dancing at a club? After drinking a beer? Smoking a cigarette? The dragon does not place concepts such as "good" or "bad" on any of these activities. Instead, she is able to engage them as part of her practice. She sees the way they affect her well-being, responds accordingly, and only engages them as much as she feels is relevant to her core motivation to be of benefit to others.

You can look to your Saturday night as a training ground. It's not a time to get sloppy drunk and lose your mind. It's a time to continue to manifest as a practitioner of mindfulness and compassion. This is the concept of tantra, or continuity. If you can hold that intention consistently, even when you're out with a group of friends, then you are off to a good start.

One small part of practicing the Vajrayana path is looking at substances that are conventionally considered harmful to your mindfulness, and seeing them as unconventional opportunities for practice. Alcoholic beverages can be seen as *amrita*, a Sanskrit word that refers to a sacramental drink. In the Catholic tradition, wine can be perceived as wine, or when it is blessed, as the blood of Jesus Christ. In a similar vein, amrita is a mixture involving water or alcohol, which is drunk as part of the idea that you can transmute seemingly negative aspects of your world into part of your path.

In this vein, Chögyam Trungpa Rinpoche used to lead his students in "mindful drinking" exercises. He would have students watch their minds as they imbibed together. The students would take a sip of alcohol, then pause and see how it affected them. Then they would take another sip. Sometimes these students engaged the practice to the point where they felt a loosening up of their ego and an unraveling of their dualistic sense of "me" versus "the world." Others threw up.

One student of Chögyam Trungpa Rinpoche said that they were encouraged to drink just enough to relax, to appreciate their situation and help their ego go to sleep. The idea was to watch how the alcohol affected them, and see how it could relax their mind. When they felt that loosening inside, then they were instructed to stop.

I would not recommend getting drunk and calling it an experiment in meditation. However, if you are serious about applying the Buddhist teachings to every aspect of your life and you occasionally have a beer, those two things do not need to be entirely separate. You can apply your mindfulness to this simple experience. You can be inquisitive about how drinking a beer affects your mind.

The point here is that when you go out on a Saturday night and you drink, have sex, or whatever, do so with an intention you believe in. If your core motivation at this point is to wake up to the world around you and act as skillfully as the dragon would, then hold firm to that regardless of what you do when you're out to play.

## Our Mistakes

There is at least one thing you have in common with every great meditation practitioner who has come before you, dating all the way back to the Buddha: you have made mistakes. The Buddha had a period in which he starved and tortured himself in the name of spirituality, and Milarepa killed dozens of people. In light of these great messes created by these great teachers, being a jerk during a bad breakup or blowing up at your roommate in anger doesn't seem so bad.

The dragon acknowledges that all is not right with the world, and still sees the magic that surrounds her. We can follow in her lead, and not be so hard on ourselves when we make mistakes and when we are not perfect practitioners. We learn from them, just like the meditation masters of the past. We can do the Milarepa. When we mess up we can acknowledge it, lighten up a bit, and reconnect with the world as it is—magical and sacred.

The first step is forgiving yourself. Knowing that everyone has made mistakes, you can rejoice in the fact that you are not alone in this regard. You can explore the feelings that surround your past indiscretions, as well as the circumstances that led to them, and learn from that process. You can then resolve not to go down the same road as you did before.

If there are people you have wronged in some way, you can seek to make amends either by speaking directly with them, or by resolving to be of benefit to others who face similar situations. From there, the only thing left to do is to let your past mistake go, and move on with your life.

We could spend our entire life dwelling on all the times we have been jerks. That seems like a waste of a lifetime to me. Instead, we need to be straightforward like the dragon, acknowledge what has come before, and move on to what is going on right now. Right now is not a mistake. Right now is magic. Allow yourself the chance to experience that magic by forgiving yourself for the past and connecting with what is going on in this very moment.

## COMPASSIONATE LEADERSHIP

The dragon is a natural leader. Because she is genuine, people trust in her ability to lead. People are magnetized to her because she exudes delight, wisdom, and confidence.

The funny thing is, the dragon didn't set out to be a leader. She just wanted to be a sane, ordinary, nice being. In the same way, you may have started your path of meditation with the goal of just getting your act together. You wanted to be calmer, and more present with your life. Through studying the qualities of the tiger, you learned how to ground yourself in the reality of this very moment. We can learn a great deal from what is going on right now. We can be gentle, precise, and discerning with whatever comes our way.

Having spent some time cultivating those qualities, your heart yearns for more. You see the suffering you have acknowledged in your own life reflected in the lives of others. You naturally feel a sense of tenderness toward them, and open up to your bodhichitta. This is the path of the snow lion: connecting with others as part of your spiritual journey. You see the suffering of your fellow coworkers, family members, and strangers on the subway, and you want to help them. You begin to manifest compassion for them, and you apply the six paramitas as tools that help you help them.

At some point you realize that your capacity for compassion goes far beyond your own preferences and concepts of who to like and how things should be. You see the simple truths of reality—that things are impermanent, and subject to change and death. Instead of giving in to the fear that comes with this realization, you address these feelings of groundlessness in a straightforward manner. You begin to see that the boundaries and set concepts you have built for the world around you are not as solid as you may have originally believed. You let the barriers around your heart dissolve, and offer your love without discrimination. From there you begin to experience equanimity.

Now you can rest in that space of equanimity. You have cultivated contentment in your daily life, joy in helping others, and an understanding of the nature of reality itself. You apply these qualities of the four dignities to your life in a real and direct way. The teachings are no longer theoretical, but are instead based in a new intimacy with your own basic goodness. You have developed confidence in your innate wisdom, and you allow it to shine forth and touch others.

You exhibit a sense of delight and humor, even in the face of large obstacles. You take whatever you encounter as an opportunity to practice the teachings. It is not philosophy at this point; it is applying the experiential understanding of your own goodness. It is manifesting an authentic presence wherever you go. It is seeing the world as sacred, and appreciating the magic of ordinary moments.

You are a master warrior already. You are already a dragon. You can realize this when you make intimate contact with your own basic goodness. You have the qualities of all four dignities inside you, waiting for you to snap out of your confusion and manifest as a genuine warrior with a heart of gold.

You are the leader this world needs. If your primary intention is to be present with your world, be compassionate with others, and be a force of positive change in the world, there is nothing holding you back. There is no one else that will clean up your life and make you happy. There is no one else who will be able to effect true change in your neighborhood like you can. There is nobody else who will offer your heart to the world and experience its sacred qualities but you. You can make a difference in this world, so long as you have confidence in your innate ability to love.

# NOTES

## Chapter 8

1. Sakyong Mipham, *Ruling Your World: Ancient Strategies for Modern Life* (New York: Morgan Road Books, 2005), p. 11.

## Chapter 11

1. Khenpo Tsultrim Gyamtso, trans., Practice 13 in *The 37 Practices of a Bodhisattva,* by Ngulchu Thogme (San Francisco: Marpa Foundation, 1994).
2. Ibid., Practice 14.
3. Ibid., Practice 15.

# RESOURCES

## Further Reading

Chödrön, Pema. *Comfortable with Uncertainty: 108 Teachings on Cultivating Fearlessness and Compassion.* Boston: Shambhala Publications, 2002.

Mipham, Sakyong. *Ruling Your World: Ancient Strategies for Modern Life.* New York: Morgan Road Books, 2005.

———. *Turning the Mind Into an Ally.* New York: Riverhead Books, 2003.

Mollod, Phineas, and Jason Tesauro. *The Modern Gentleman: A Guide to Essential Manners, Savvy, and Vice.* Berkeley: Ten Speed Press, 2002.

Nichtern, Ethan. *One City: A Declaration of Interdependence.* Somerville, Mass.: Wisdom Publications, 2007.

Spider-Man comics from Marvel.

Thogme, Ngulchu. *The 37 Practices of a Bodhisattva.* San Francisco: The Marpa Foundation, 1994.

Trungpa, Chögyam. *Shambhala: The Sacred Path of the Warrior.* Boston: Shambhala Publications, 1984.

## MEDITATION PROGRAMS

The Way of Shambhala is an in-depth exploration of the four dignities of Shambhala and how they link to the three yanas, or vehicles, of Tibetan Buddhism. It is a combination of weekend retreats (Shambhala Training Levels) and weekly classes. I couldn't recommend it enough.

The Way of Shambhala is offered at Shambhala Meditation Centers worldwide.

## WEBSITES

www.shambhala.org
www.lodrorinzler.com